War Of The Words
25 Years Of Super Bowl
Head-Butts And High-Fives
Quote By Quote

Compiled And Edited By

Wes Janz & Vickie Abrahamson

Bobbleheads Press, Inc.
Minneapolis, Minnesota

<u>War Of The Words: 25 Years Of Super Bowl Head-Butts And High-Fives, Quote By Quote</u>

© 1991 Wes Janz and Vickie Abrahamson

Bobbleheads Press, Inc.
420 North Fifth Street, Suite 570
Minneapolis, Minnesota 55401 USA
(612) 338-1005

Printed in the United States of America
First Printing, November 1991

Library of Congress Catalog Card Number 91-77226
ISBN Number: 0-9630330-2-6

<u>War Of The Words</u> Series
Editors: Wes Janz and Vickie Abrahamson
Book Design: Marcia Stone

<u>25 Years Of Super Bowl Head-Butts And High-Fives, Quote By Quote</u>
Editors: Wes Janz and Vickie Abrahamson
Chief Editorial Assistant: Jana Branch
Additional Editorial Assistance: John Weibusch and Phil Barber, National Football League Properties, Inc.
Illustration and Art Direction: Jerry Stenback
Typesetting: Roxanne Thoeny

Material compiled in this publication was gathered through research of a number of sources, including the following:

Magazine Sources:
Sports Illustrated, Time, U.S. News & World Report

Newspaper Sources:
Daily Olympian, Los Angeles Times, Miami Herald, Minneapolis StarTribune, Minneapolis Tribune, New Orleans Times-Picayune, New York Times, Sporting News, St. Paul Dispatch, St. Paul Pioneer Press-Dispatch, USA Today, Washington Post

Book Sources:
National Football League Publications
Official Super Bowl XXV Game Program
The Official National Football League 1991 Record & Fact Book
The Super Bowl: Celebrating a Quarter-Century of America's Greatest Game
The First Fifty Years: A Celebration of the National Football League in its Fiftieth Season

National Football Museum, Inc. publication
The Pro Football Hall of Fame 1991-1992 Souvenir Yearbook

Pro Football Hall of Fame publication
Pro Football Hall of Fame: The Story Behind the Dream

Acknowledgments

This book would still be a Super Bowl dream if it were not for the exuberant teamwork of these key players: Marcia Stone, *War Of The Words* book designer; researchers Bruce Morgan, David Aafedt and Dean Janz; Jana Branch, Jerry Stenback and Roxanne Thoeny for design and production expertise; our special team at Ambassador Press: Barry Engle, Clark Underthun, Bud Gilbertson and Mike Moreland; Pat "The Bottom Line" Aafedt for energized vision; and Harvey Mackay, author of *Swim With the Sharks Without Being Eaten Alive* – our favorite wild-card pick in any game.

And a special high-five to Tom Richardson, John Wiebusch, Phil Barber, Sandy Giornali and Tom Snelling of National Football League Properties. We'd like to carry you guys off the field on our shoulders. This book wouldn't have made it to the end zone without you.

Contents

Introduction

I've been dreaming Super Bowl dreams since before that first big game in Los Angeles Coliseum when the American Football League squared off against the National Football League. No, in 1967, I never thought it could get this big. Especially when the first game had 32,000 empty seats. Fortunately, that was the first and only time we didn't have a sellout. In fact, the Super Bowl ticket is the most coveted seat in American sports. Fans bought tickets for the first game scaled at $12, $10, and $6. It's all relative, I know, but for the last five years game tickets have been priced as high as $150 (and often resold for many times face value). It is fair to say that every January the eyes of the world are focused on this amazing event.

From the beginning, some of the press tagged the AFL-NFL World Championship Game the "Super Bowl." The actual source of "Super" in the Super Bowl name originated with the daughter of Lamar Hunt, the Chiefs' owner. At that time, a popular, faddish children's toy was something called a "Super Ball," which bounced dramatically higher than a regular rubber ball. Lamar's daughter had one of those balls and he liked the name—the twist of "Super Ball" to "Super Bowl"—and he urged we adopt it. Thankfully we did, and the third game became Super Bowl III.

A lot of things were different then than they are today. In the early years, I remember sitting around shooting the breeze with six, seven, eight writers at a time. It seemed to be less serious then, more fun. The game was serious, of

By Pete Rozelle

course, but that didn't keep us from kidding around. Nowadays, thousands of media people from around the world cover the game and the closest the commissioner gets to these people is at the giant Friday noon press conference where there's a bank of TV cameras and hundreds of reporters.

Each Super Bowl holds its own special memories in my heart. To recall just a few–the greater-than-great Vince Lombardi leading his Packers to victory in games I and II; Joe Namath's confident "guarantee" of a Jets victory over the heavily favored Baltimore Colts; presenting the game trophy to an all-deserving Art Rooney in the Steelers' first appearance in the Super Bowl after more than four decades of trying to get there; the Bears' Jim McMahon's sporting a headband emblazoned with "ROZELLE" in the playoffs before Super Bowl XX, after I had banned the wearing of commercial headbands; and Herb Alpert's "pure" horn version of the National Anthem in XXII.

All in all, it has been a great, great ride–from Super Bowl I through my last game as Commissioner at XXIII to now. I wish I literally could release some balloons and doves at this point, and maybe even arrange for a fly-over for everyone reading this book. You'll have to use your imagination, however. Or better, like me, keep dreaming Super Bowl dreams.

TEAMS OF THE
American Football Conference

Buffalo
Bills

Cincinnati
Bengals

Cleveland
Browns

Denver
Broncos

Houston
Oilers

Indianapolis
Colts

Kansas City
Chiefs

Los Angeles
Raiders

Miami
Dolphins

New England
Patriots

New York
Jets

Pittsburgh
Steelers

San Diego
Chargers

Seattle
Seahawks

TEAMS OF THE
National Football Conference

Atlanta
Falcons

Chicago
Bears

Dallas
Cowboys

Detroit
Lions

Green Bay
Packers

Los Angeles
Rams

Minnesota
Vikings

New Orleans
Saints

New York
Giants

Philadelphia
Eagles

Phoenix
Cardinals

San Francisco
49ers

Tampa Bay
Buccaneers

Washington
Redskins

War Of The Words
25 Years Of Super Bowl Head-Butts And High-Fives Quote By Quote

*An officially licensed product
of the National Football League.*

Super Bowl I

GAME SUMMARY

January 15, 1967
Memorial Coliseum
Los Angeles, California

The NFL Packers scored the first Super Bowl points on a 37-yard pass from game MVP Bart Starr to wide receiver Max McGee, a veteran who had made only 4 catches during the regular season.
The AFL Chiefs got their first points on a 7-yard pass from Len Dawson to running back Curtis McClinton. Green Bay scored 21 points in the second half, including Willie Wood's 50-yard interception return.

We're gonna whip Green Bay's rear.

Fred
(The Hammer)
Williamson
Kansas City cornerback

We were scared to death .... guys in the tunnel were throwing up and wetting their pants.

E.J. Holub
Kansas City linebacker

There is no way the Green Bay Packers are going to lose this football game.

Vince Lombardi
Green Bay head coach

At that time, it was one league against the other league. We really wanted to clobber the AFL.

Elijah Pitts
Green Bay running back, remembering the first Super Bowl on its 25th anniversary in 1991

Green Bay Packers	7	7	14	7	**35**
Kansas City Chiefs	0	10	0	0	**10**

Head Coaches Vince Lombardi, Hank Stram
MVP Bart Starr *Green Bay quarterback*

We knew Coach Lombardi was getting phone calls from Coach Halas, from Wellington Mara, and they did not just want a win—they wanted a thrashing.

Jerry Kramer
Green Bay guard, referring to Halas, the Chicago Bears' head coach and owner, and to Mara, the New York Giants' owner

Vince was like a man possessed. He really felt that if we lost, a lot of what we had accomplished [4 NFL titles before the first Super Bowl] would be tarnished … Most of all, we didn't want to let him down.

Bob Skoronski
Green Bay offensive tackle

The movable pocket will be the football of the '70s.

Hank Stram
Kansas City head coach, on the Chiefs' offensive alignment

Formations do not win football games. Blocking and tackling does.

Vince Lombardi
Green Bay head coach

SIDELINE

The name "Super Bowl" was coined by Lamar Hunt, owner of the Kansas City Chiefs, after hearing his son and daughter rave about their Wham-O Super Balls. The league did not promote the name initially because, according to Hunt, Commissioner Pete Rozelle thought the name was undignified.

Green Bay wide receiver Boyd Dowler was the first person introduced at the Super Bowl and the first one hurt.

3 0   3 5   4 0   4 5

Super Bowl I

The weapon of weaklings...

Vince Lombardi
Green Bay head coach, describing the blitz

During the five minutes or so we talked, [Lombardi] held onto my arm, and he was shaking like a leaf. It was incredible.

Frank Gifford
Television announcer, on his interview with Vince Lombardi before the game

I'll drop the hammer on him. Two hammers on Dowler and one on Dale should be enough. Bart Starr. Who's he anyway?

Fred (The Hammer) Williamson
Kansas City cornerback, referring to the Green Bay wide receivers and quarterback

Back on the sideline, Fuzzy Thurston asked me, 'Did you get him?' and I said 'No.' He asked Gale Gillingham, ... and Gilly said 'No,' so Fuzzy said, 'I guess Donny hit him with his purse.'

Jerry Kramer
Green Bay guard, recounting the play in which Green Bay running back Donny Anderson knocked Fred Williamson unconscious (Fuzzy Thurston stood over Williamson before he was carried off the field and hummed softly, "If I Had a Hammer...")

I pointed to one of the officials and Starr said to me, 'Norm, isn't he one of ours?'

Norm Schacter
Game referee, on Green Bay quarterback Bart Starr's response when he learned that a penalty on the Packers had been called by one of the three NFL officials working the game with three AFL officials

40   35   30   25

Attendance	61,946
Top Ticket Price	$12
TV Average Share	78 *refers to the percentage of households using televisions during the telecast that tuned in to the game*

It's impossible for me to believe that those balding old men on the Packers could have handled us with such ridiculous ease.

Jerry Mays
Kansas City
defensive end

I was so surprised that I expected to open my other hand and find a silver dollar.

Max McGee
Green Bay receiver,
on his one-handed
touchdown catch

I came in second best in the love department. His first love was his precious Packers.

Marie Lombardi
remembering her
husband's passion
for his team

The game ball ... the players gave it to me. It's the NFL ball. It catches better and kicks a little better than the AFL ball.

Vince Lombardi
Green Bay
head coach

END ZONE

Each member of the championship team received $15,000; each member of the losing team took home $7,500. These amounts did not change until Super Bowl XII.

Steep ticket prices were blamed for the 32,000 empty seats in the Coliseum. Ticket scalpers sold an $8 seat for $2. Every other Super Bowl has had sellout attendance.

Both the NFL ball, nicknamed "The Duke," and the AFL ball were used in game I.

Super Bowl II

GAME SUMMARY

January 14, 1968
Orange Bowl
Miami, Florida

Green Bay's Don Chandler kicked 4 field goals, and Bart Starr and wide receiver Boyd Dowler connected on a 62-yard scoring pass. The Packers' Herb Adderley clinched the victory when he returned a fourth quarter interception 60 yards for a touchdown. MVP Bart Starr completed 13 of 24 passes for 202 yards.

Mrs. Lombardi: God, your feet are cold.

Mr. Lombardi: When we are alone, you may call me Vince, dear.

Fabled exchange between Marie and Vince Lombardi in bed one night

The whole world is NFL-oriented ... You know playing the Packers is like playing our fathers.

Bill Budness
Oakland linebacker

The history of the Packers is in the future, not in the past.

Vince Lombardi
Green Bay head coach

Green Bay Packers	3	13	10	7	**33**
Oakland Raiders	0	7	0	7	**14**

Head Coaches Vince Lombardi, John Rauch

MVP Bart Starr *Green Bay quarterback*

We'll just stick our noses in there. That's our game. Seek and destroy ... [laughter] ... That sounds as corny as 'run to daylight.'

Dan Connors

Oakland linebacker, referring to Lombardi's offensive philosophy and the title of his autobiography

This is the Super Bowl! You guys are disgusting!

Al Davis

Oakland managing general partner, to reporters whose attention was diverted during a press conference by a bikini-clad woman descending a staircase

Al Davis was a darling, just a cute kid.

Esther Gillman

wife of San Diego Chargers head coach Sid Gillman (Since Davis joined the Raiders in 1963, they have been the winningest franchise in pro football.)

I don't give a damn what they look like as long as they go over.

Don Chandler

Green Bay placekicker, on his 4 field goals and 3 extra points

SIDELINE

Pregame ceremonies featured a battle between two 30-foot papier mâché models of a Raider and a Packer. They were moved toward each other on the field, their arms pumping slowly while steam spouted from their heads. Unfortunately, the steam was gone before the battle began.

CBS paid $2.5 million to televise Super Bowl II.

Super Bowl II

Cannon: Okay, I'm holding a gun to your head and you've got to answer the question. The question is, what do you do more, run or pass? Remember, there's a gun to your head.

Rauch: I'd say we try to balance our offense.

Cannon: BANG!!

Exchange between writer Jimmy Cannon and Oakland head coach John Rauch, who was known for his indirect answers

On paper, I don't think they are any better than us.

Tom Keating
Oakland defensive tackle

Where the hell did everybody go?

John Rauch
Oakland head coach, on the sideline when Green Bay's Boyd Dowler was not covered and caught a 62-yard touchdown pass

The Packers never change. They just come at you and beat you.

Billy Cannon
Oakland tight end

It was typical of the way we've played all year. We get a 13- or 14-point lead and then we go on vacation.

Vince Lombardi
Green Bay head coach

It was a day of learning; I learned an awful lot.

Daryle Lamonica
Oakland quarterback

If we played them every day of the week, we'd split.

Dan Birdwell
Oakland defensive tackle

40   35   30   25

Attendance	75,546
Top Ticket Price	$12
TV Average Share	68

They were just big, quick, and smart.

Ben Davidson
Oakland defensive end

The harder you work, the harder it is to surrender.

Vince Lombardi
Green Bay head coach

I just can't imagine us throwing Coach Lombardi in the shower.

Marv Fleming
Green Bay tight end

Next year, I dare say, it'll go right down to the wire.

Henry Jordan
Green Bay defensive tackle, referring to the improving competition offered by AFL teams

This is the best way to leave a football field.

Vince Lombardi
Green Bay head coach, to offensive linemen Forrest Gregg and Jerry Kramer as they carried him off the field on their shoulders

END ZONE

Going into Super Bowl II, the Packers were coming off their legendary win over Dallas in the "Ice Bowl" where the field had been frozen slick and the players had endured -46° windchill.

Game MVP Bart Starr was a 17th round draft choice in 1956.

Super Bowl II was Vince Lombardi's last game as head coach of the Packers. In his last 7 years, the Packers won more than 75% of their games and 5 NFL championships.

15   10   5

Super Bowl III

GAME SUMMARY

January 12, 1969
Orange Bowl
Miami, Florida

*B*altimore brought a 15-1 regular season record into the game and was an overwhelming favorite. The Jets were led by game MVP Joe Namath, who completed 17 of 28 passes for 206 yards. Colts quarterback Earl Morrall was intercepted 3 times in the first half. Johnny Unitas came off the bench to lead the Colts to their only touchdown–a 1-yard run by running back Jerry Hill.

Colts, 47-0.

Tex Maule
Sports Illustrated
pre-game pick

*T*he whole world's against you. They're laughing at you.

Weeb Ewbank
New York head coach,
to his players, as quoted
by Jets placekicker
Jim Turner

*W*e never recognized the American Football League ... it was just a semi-pro league. If you couldn't make it in the NFL that's where you went.

Alex Hawkins
Baltimore receiver

New York Jets	0	7	6	3	**16**
Baltimore Colts	0	0	0	7	**7**

Head Coaches	Weeb Ewbank, Don Shula
MVP	Joe Namath *New York quarterback*

We're gonna win the game. I'll guarantee you.

Joe Namath

New York quarterback, to patrons at the Miami Touchdown Club including members of the Baltimore Colts

Ah, Joe, Joe. They're gonna put that on the locker room wall. Those Colts are gonna want to kill us.

Weeb Ewbank
New York head coach

Someday he'll learn a little humility.

Billy Ray Smith

Baltimore defensive lineman, on Joe Namath

What we like about [Namath] is that he is a winner. He doesn't know about losing.

Weeb Ewbank
New York head coach

I'm not that crazy...

Joe Namath

New York quarterback on reports that he and Colts defensive end Lou Michaels had been in a fight

Wives can do a bed check a heck of a lot better than I can.

Weeb Ewbank
New York head coach, on why players should bring their spouses to the Super Bowl

SIDELINE

Super Bowl III was the first game to officially carry the name "Super Bowl." The previous two contests were known as the "AFL-NFL World Championship Game." The media liked "Super Bowl" and after the third contest the name stuck.

Apollo 8 astronauts Frank Borman, James Lovell and William Anders, recently returned from their lunar orbit, led the crowd in the Pledge of Allegiance.

30   35   40   45

Super Bowl III

They said he could never do it .... They said he was boasting, but I knew he wasn't. I said they'd win by ten points. He made a liar out of me. They won by nine.

John Namath
Joe's father

It was a whale of a ball game, Joseph–and you're a whale of a ball player, sideburns, fur-carpeted pad and all.

Bill Boni
to Joe Namath in the St. Paul Dispatch

This is the start of a new era in pro football.

Weeb Ewbank
New York head coach

She never comes. Her nerves won't stand it–she swells up like a balloon.

Joe Namath
New York quarterback, on why his mother didn't attend any of his big games

Dear Ted: You can't win them all. Best wishes, Nelson

Nelson Rockefeller
Governor of New York, in a telegram to Spiro [Ted] Agnew, Vice President-elect and former Governor of Maryland

Better him than me. Do you think anyone would be crying for me now if the Colts had won? Hah!

Joe Namath
New York quarterback, when asked if he felt sorry for Baltimore quarterback Earl Morrall

Attendance	75,389
Top Ticket Price	$12
TV Average Share	70

The Super Bowl is a world theater. The world is a happening. In the speed-up of the electronic age, we want things to happen. This offers us a mosaic that the fans love– everything is in action at once.

Marshall McLuhan
Educator-philosopher

What I remember is Pat Summerall crying next to the Colts' locker room after the game …. the Colts wouldn't let him in after they lost. For NFL people, it was a big blow for their team to lose. Tears were streaming down his face.

Ted Nathanson
NBC football coordinating producer, remembering, in 1989, Super Bowl III

If I live to be 97, there won't be a week I don't think about it. We were the first NFL team to be humiliated before the world.

Bill Curry
Baltimore center

END ZONE

Weeb Ewbank's two artificial hips are reminders of the season that culminated in Super Bowl III. He was injured twice that season, once while getting a victory ride and again when he was thrown in a locker room shower during the Super Bowl celebration.

With a total of two touchdowns, the Jets and Colts set a Super Bowl record for fewest touchdowns for both teams.

The Road To The Super Bowl

AFL – NFL Playoffs 1966-67 *(2 out of 15 NFL teams and 2 out of 9 AFL teams vie for the World Championship)*

National Football League

League Championship

World Championship

Eastern Conference Champion

Dallas (10-3-1)

Green Bay

Western Conference Champion

Green Bay (12-2)

American Football League

Eastern Division Champion

Buffalo (9-4-1)

Kansas City

Western Division Champion

Kansas City (11-2-1)

NFL Playoffs 1990-91 *(12 out of 28 teams vie for the Super Bowl)*

National Football Conference

First Round	Divisional Playoff	Championship	Super Bowl

Wild Card #1
Philadelphia (10-6)

Washington

Wild Card #2
Washington (10-6)

San Francisco

Division Champion #1
San Francisco (14-2)

New York

Division Champion #2
New York Giants (13-3)

New York

Division Champion #3
Chicago (11-5)

Chicago

Wild Card #3
New Orleans (8-8)

American Football Conference

Wild Card #1
Miami (12-4)

Miami

Wild Card #2
Kansas City (11-5)

Buffalo

Division Champion #1
Buffalo (13-3)

Buffalo

Division Champion #2
LA Raiders (12-4)

Los Angeles

Division Champion #3
Cincinnati (9-7)

Cincinnati

Wild Card #3
Houston (9-7)

Super Bowl IV

GAME SUMMARY

January 11, 1970
Tulane Stadium
New Orleans, Louisiana

Kansas City's defense dominated, intercepting 3 passes and sacking Minnesota quarterback Joe Kapp 3 times. All of Minnesota's fourth-quarter possessions ended in interceptions. Chiefs placekicker Jan Stenerud contributed 3 field goals.

C'mon, Lenny, pump it in there, baby. Just keep matriculating the ball down the field, boys!

Hank Stram
Kansas City head coach, shouting from the sidelines

Any quarterback who can knock Jim Houston cold is all man.

Buck Buchanan
Kansas City defensive tackle, after Minnesota quarterback Joe Kapp knocked out Cleveland linebacker Jim Houston in the NFC Championship Game

Most quarterbacks look for somewhere to run out of bounds. Mine looks for someone to run into.

Bud Grant
Minnesota head coach, on quarterback Joe Kapp

Kansas City Chiefs	3	13	7	0	**23**
Minnesota Vikings	0	0	7	0	**7**

Head Coaches	Hank Stram, Bud Grant
MVP	Len Dawson *Kansas City quarterback*

I was a little crazy, but I wasn't insane. I might try to bowl over a linebacker once in a while. But as a rule, you don't survive if you try that stuff regularly.

Joe Kapp
Minnesota quarterback, recalling Super Bowl IV

My eyes were really burning. You watch a lot of film as a coach.

Hank Stram
Kansas City head coach, remembering the morning of game day

You are always more motivated by the fact you didn't succeed the first time.

Hank Stram
Kansas City head coach, on the effect that losing in Super Bowl I had on the Chiefs

I thought about trying to go back to sleep. Then the nausea came again.

Len Dawson
Kansas City quarterback remembering the morning of the Super Bowl and the pressure he felt

SIDELINE

Halftime featured a re-enactment of the Battle of New Orleans of 1812. Cannons were blasted, smoke spread through the stadium, and while many coughed and rubbed their eyes, men with muskets fell in mock death on the field. A pregame hot air balloon battle was pre-empted when one of the balloons sailed into the stands. The balloonist, George Stokes, was costumed as a Viking and recalled, "There was no sympathy, not even laughter. The crowd was ugly. It started ripping my balloon apart ..."

Super Bowl IV

I don't know that it constituted a Presidential pardon, but it sure made Leonard feel better.

Hank Stram

Kansas City head coach after a call from President Richard Nixon to wish the team well and to tell quarterback Len Dawson not to worry about allegations of gambling illegalities that had captured most media coverage during the week

I was hungry. I was always hungry. Hungry for it all. First, breakfast. Then the world championship.

Joe Kapp

Minnesota quarterback, recalling the morning of game day

This is the first time I've heard this. I know we paid for a lot of meals.

Hank Stram

Kansas City head coach, after hearing a player comment that he was so nervous before the game that he didn't eat for three days

It lit us all up. We knew what it meant.

Willie Lanier

Kansas City linebacker, recalling the "AFL-10" patch sewn on their jerseys to commemorate the league's tenth and final year

Just play better.

Bud Grant

Minnesota head coach's advice to his players when they were down 13-0

I don't believe I've ever seen anyone kick the ball so well, so high.

Jerry Burns

Minnesota's offensive coordinator, on Kansas City's kickers

Attendance	80,562
Top Ticket Price	$15
TV Average Share	69

There wasn't any doubt that the better team won. The Kansas City defense looked like a redwood forest.

Joe Kapp
Minnesota quarterback

I was so tense, I can hardly remember.

Jan Stenerud
Kansas City placekicker, when asked how he thought he had played

Those guys [the Vikings] look like they're in a Chinese fire drill.

Hank Stram
Kansas City head coach, on Minnesota's outplayed defensive unit

It simply wasn't the end of the world to lose that game to Kansas City. What's older than yesterday's newspaper? The Super Bowl is one game, for the highest stakes, and that appeals to America. But losing that game isn't like dying.

Bud Grant
Vikings head coach, remembering Super Bowl IV

END ZONE

On the Sunday of Super Bowl IV, Kansas City police reported just one burglary. They waited until halftime to question the suspect, who asked the first question – "What's the score?"

The Vikings' battle cry "40 for 60" meant that every player must give his all at every moment of the game.

15   10   5

Super Bowl V

GAME SUMMARY

January 17, 1971
Orange Bowl
Miami, Florida

The "Blunder Bowl" featured 7 turnovers by the Colts and 4 by the Cowboys. The Cowboys were also penalized for 133 yards. An interception by Colt linebacker Mike Curtis set up rookie placekicker Jim O'Brien's winning field goal with only 5 seconds on the game clock.

God that memory hurts. But maybe it toughened us. I used to puke before every game and now I don't anymore.

Carroll Rosenbloom

Baltimore owner, on the impact of the Colts' loss at Super Bowl III

This one will be an emotional bath .... Both teams know the bitterness and frustration of losing the big game. But here we have the edge .... The money is unimportant. I want the ring.

Mike Curtis
Baltimore linebacker

Baltimore Colts	0	6	0	10	**16**
Dallas Cowboys	3	10	0	0	**13**

Head Coaches Don McCafferty, Tom Landry
MVP Chuck Howley *Dallas linebacker*

The money makes it different.

Johnny Unitas
Baltimore quarterback

He can only improve.

Sid Gillman
San Diego Chargers head coach, on Dallas quarterback Craig Morton

We're not in the toilet bowl this time.

Leroy Jordan
Dallas linebacker, referring to the Playoff Bowl, a now-defunct consolation game

I should have caught it. College kids can catch the easy ones. The ones you get paid for catching are the hard ones.

Dan Reeves
Dallas running back, on a dropped pass that resulted in a Baltimore interception

A year ago I was sitting in a frat house at Clemson watching the Super Bowl.

Charlie Waters
Dallas rookie safety

I was actually embarrassed to come back out of the locker room [after halftime].

Bob Vogel
Baltimore offensive tackle

SIDELINE

Super Bowl V was the first to be designated with a roman numeral. The numerals were grandfathered back to the first four games.

Cowboys linebacker Chuck Howley is the only member of a losing team to be named game MVP.

Four Air Force jets that were scheduled to fly over the stadium during the national anthem arrived two minutes after the last note was played.

30   35   40   45

Super Bowl V

I hope I don't make that many mistakes in one day.

Richard Nixon
President of the United States, on the game's 11 turnovers

I haven't been around many games where the players hit harder. Sometimes people watch a game … and they talk about how sloppy the play was. The mistakes in that game weren't invented, at least not by the people who made them. Most were forced.

Tom Landry
Dallas head coach

When we broke the huddle, Jim was trying to pull up grass blades and throw them to check the wind. I reminded him we were on artificial turf.

Earl Morrall
Baltimore quarterback and holder, on placekicker Jim O'Brien's state of mind before the winning field goal

Frustration. I did it out of frustration.

Bob Lilly
Dallas defensive tackle, on why he tossed his helmet 50 yards downfield after the Cowboys were defeated

At least the TV watchers could have escaped if they so desired. The folks here were trapped.

Arthur Daley
New York Times

Attendance	79,204
Top Ticket Price	$15
TV Average Share	75

I had a dream last week .... I dreamt that somebody kicked a long field goal to win the Super Bowl game. I didn't know if it was [Dallas kicker] Mike Clark or myself. I told the players on the team about it and they laughed.

Jim O'Brien
Baltimore placekicker, reflecting on his winning field goal with 5 seconds remaining in the game

*I'*m an Aquarian, and this is my age.

Jim O'Brien
Baltimore placekicker, who was nicknamed "Lassie" because of his long hair

*T*his will be my last game unless I turn referee.

Billy Ray Smith
Baltimore defensive tackle

Perhaps the game should be called the Blunder Bowl from now on .... And to think television was worried that situation comedy was dead.

Tex Maule
Sports Illustrated

END ZONE

Baltimore's Don McCafferty was the first rookie head coach to take a team to the Super Bowl and win. The 49ers' George Seifert did it next in Super Bowl XXIV.

Tom Landry, Dallas Cowboys head coach 1960-1988, holds the NFL record for most regular-season games lost with 162. He is, however, in good company: George Halas is next with 148, followed by Chuck Noll with 139 (at the start of the 1991 season).

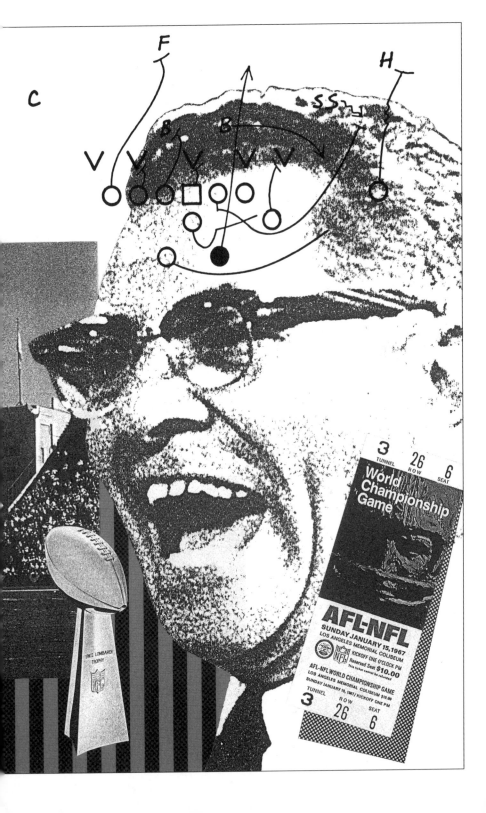

Super Bowl VI

GAME SUMMARY

January 16, 1972
Tulane Stadium
New Orleans, Louisiana

Dallas running backs led the Cowboy assault–Duane Thomas with 95 yards and Walt Garrison with 74. Wide receiver Lance Alworth and tight end Mike Ditka each caught 7-yard scoring passes from game MVP Roger Staubach.

If it's the ultimate, how come they're playing it again next year?

Duane Thomas
Dallas running back, referring to the Super Bowl

Just another game, but one that happens to be the only game in the world.

Bob Griese
Miami quarterback, on the Super Bowl

You know how players are. Always gotta try something new or different. I mean, like little kids, you know?

Mike Ditka
Dallas tight end explaining how tackle Ralph Neely broke his leg riding dirt bikes off-road with Ditka and running back Dan Reeves

Dallas Cowboys	3	7	7	7	**24**
Miami Dolphins	0	3	0	0	**3**

Head Coaches	Tom Landry, Don Shula
MVP	Roger Staubach *Dallas quarterback*

I think you can hit Paul Warfield in that down-and-in pattern.

Richard Nixon
President of the United States, to Miami head coach Don Shula

*I'*d rather take Billy's prayers. I know they will be better than any play [Nixon] has.

Tom Landry
Dallas head coach, (known to some as Pope Landry I) referring to his friend, evangelist Billy Graham

*E*vidently.

Duane Thomas
Dallas running back, when asked if opponents were surprised by his speed

I hate to say it, but a quarterback who plays that way gets hurt sooner or later. I guess he doesn't want to play too long.

Dave Wilcox
San Francisco 49ers linebacker, on the scrambling style of Dallas quarterback Roger Staubach

*T*hey were tough football players. I mean, really tough. These fellows had been down, they'd been kicked around, they'd been criticized, they'd been made fun of …. that made them very tough-minded people.

Tom Landry
Dallas head coach, reflecting on the character of his 1971 Cowboys

SIDELINE

Don Shula is the only head coach to take more than one team to the Super Bowl–the Colts and the Dolphins. Even more impressive, he has made those trips in three different decades–the 1960s, 1970s and 1980s. His six-game total (2-4) is a record among coaches.

30   35   40   45

Super Bowl VI

They ran it down our throats.

Bill Stanfill
Miami defensive end

They came to win and we came to play.

Eugene (Mercury) Morris
Miami running back

One thing we did to confuse them was to be less confusing.

Mike Ditka
Dallas tight end

A disaster.

Don Shula
Miami head coach

Why'd we lose? We started to question ourselves and then we tried to do more than we were prepared for .... It's when everything goes south on you.

Howard Twilley
Miami wide receiver

We'll be back. This was just a start. They can't say we don't win the big ones anymore .... I am looking forward to a dynasty like the New York Yankees and the Boston Celtics.

Tex Schramm
Dallas general manager,
(Dallas was 1-1 in the
next six Super Bowls)

I don't see why we can't have a dynasty like Green Bay had. I say that providing I am still here.

Mike Ditka
Dallas tight end,
who retired after the
1972 season

40   35   30   25

Attendance	81,023
Top Ticket Price	$15
TV Average Share	74

All this year everything was a step toward this day. I feel like I've walked uphill the last six years and just reached the top.

Bob Lilly
Dallas defensive tackle

It was just the successful conclusion of our twelve-year plan.

Clint Murchison
Owner of the Dallas Cowboys explaining the Super Bowl win

We learned one thing–when it's over, it's over. All week, we had media people up to our ears. But once that game was over the media just wanted to talk to one team, and it wasn't us.

Howard Twilley
Miami wide receiver

END ZONE

The Miami Dolphins reached the Super Bowl just six years after being granted their franchise by the NFL.

The 3 points scored by the Dolphins is the lowest total ever recorded by a Super Bowl participant.

The first 25 Super Bowls had a combined attendance of 2,027,503.

Super Bowl VII

GAME SUMMARY

January 14, 1973
Memorial Coliseum
Los Angeles, California

Miami completed the only undefeated and untied season in NFL history with this victory. The Redskins' only score occurred late in the fourth quarter when they blocked a Garo Yepremian field-goal attempt. Yepremian picked up the football and fumbled as he tried to pass. The ball was scooped up by Washington's Mike Bass, who returned it for a touchdown. MVP Miami safety Jake Scott had 2 interceptions.

Okay, Jim, which one are we gonna lose? We gotta lose one game or else we'll jinx ourselves for the playoffs. Nobody goes undefeated in the NFL.

Bob Kuechenberg
Miami guard, in a conversation with center Jim Langer late in the season

Coach Shula said our objective is not to look back at what happened at [Super Bowl VI] but now go forward and strive for perfection. And he said that boils down to taking a game at a time and winning every game.

Larry Csonka
Miami running back

Miami Dolphins	7	7	0	0	**14**
Washington Redskins	0	0	0	7	**7**

Head Coaches Don Shula, George Allen
MVP Jake Scott *Miami safety*

The future is now.

George Allen

Washington head coach, on trading away future draft choices and younger players for older, experienced players (his team was nicknamed the "Over-the-Hill Gang")

I gave George an unlimited budget and he's already exceeded it.

Edward Bennett Williams

Washington owner on George Allen's extravagance

George Allen said ... that his team had never lost a game when it was raining. So if it does rain on Sunday, we plan to forfeit.

Don Shula

Miami head coach in a sarcastic reply to the Washington head coach's solicitous comments about the Dolphins

---

I think someone was expecting the Dallas Cowboys to be here. Nobody respects my bunch of old-timers, my Over-the-Hill Gang.

George Allen

Washington head coach, after the team was greeted at the practice field by blue and white shoes and duffel bags (Dallas team colors) for each player

---

SIDELINE

Georgetown University Hospital installed television sets in the labor rooms of the maternity ward to accommodate fathers-to-be who previously delayed bringing their wives in until the Super Bowl game– and in some cases the postgame show– had ended.

The Apollo 16 crew and their re-entry-blackened capsule made an appearance at Super Bowl VII.

30　　35　　40　　45

Super Bowl VII

To win this game, I'd let you stick a knife in me and draw all my blood.

George Allen
Washington head coach

The two superlatives that team had were pride and intelligence. And, oh yeah, Don Shula.

Larry Csonka
Miami running back describing his team

We had a lot of rebel people on that team. There was a lot of turmoil. There was complaining everywhere except on the field.

Jim Kiick
Miami running back, on his team

Super Bowl rings have special powers .... Win one of these and you're the best. To win it all ... man, you've just got to know what it's like.

Marv Fleming
Miami tight end showing his teammates one of his two Super Bowl rings won with the Green Bay Packers

No one believes me, but I have a very good arm.

Garo Yepremian
Miami placekicker

There was not a juror in South Florida who would have convicted Shula for horse-whipping his kicker.

George Vecsey
New York Times

40   35   30   25

Attendance	90,182
Top Ticket Price	$15
TV Average Share	72

This is the first time the goat of the game is in the winner's locker room.

Garo Yepremian

Miami placekicker, on throwing his blocked field goal attempt to Washington's Mike Bass who converted it into a 49-yard run– Washington's only touchdown

I don't know what I'm going to tell 'em when training camp opens.

Don Shula

Miami head coach, referring to the Dolphins' 17-0-0 season and his concern about motivating the team further

We're Numero Uno!

Francisco Garcia

Miami resident, Cuban exile and Dolphins fan

I mean, nobody's perfect, right? But we were. For one season, we sure were.

Larry Csonka

Miami running back

END ZONE

9 of the top 10 television broadcasts, determined by Nielsen ratings, are Super Bowls, the only exception being the last episode of M*A*S*H. Seventeen of the top twenty broadcasts are Super Bowls.

Miami's unbeaten season also set an NFL record for most consecutive regular-season victories (14). The Chicago Bears won 13 in 1934 and the 1985 Bears and 1969 Minnesota Vikings each won 12.

15   10   5

Super Bowl VIII

GAME SUMMARY

January 13, 1974
Rice Stadium
Houston, Texas

Miami scored touchdowns on its first two possessions against the Vikings' "Purple People Eaters Defense." Minnesota ran only six offensive plays in the first quarter as the Dolphins' "No-Name Defense" dominated the game. MVP Larry Csonka rushed 33 times for 145 yards.

What did she expect? She knew the game was on.

A relative commenting on a woman's complaint that no one attended her baby's baptism

I wouldn't say that the Dolphins are bored. It just isn't the great exciting adventure it was the first two times around.

Don Shula

Miami head coach, on the Dolphins' third consecutive trip to the Super Bowl

This is the Super Bowl, not a pickup game .... I don't think our players have seen anything like this since junior high school.

Bud Grant

Minnesota head coach complaining about the practice facilities the Vikings were assigned

Look for the team that complains first. That team will lose. It never fails.

John Madden

Raiders coach whose prediction regarding the Vikings became known as John Madden's Law

Miami Dolphins	14	3	7	0	**24**
Minnesota Vikings	0	0	0	7	**7**

Head Coaches Don Shula, Bud Grant
MVP Larry Csonka *Miami running back*

Last year you guys were glaring at me thinking, 'There's old Zero and Two shooting the stuff to us.' If I get even, I might get some respect.

Don Shula
Miami head coach

I remember being shocked at the sloth and moral degeneracy of the Nixon press corps during the 1972 Presidential campaign. But they were like a pack of wolverines on speed compared to the relatively elite sports-writers who showed up in Houston ...

Hunter Thompson
Rolling Stone

It's frustrating to chase him when he is scrambling .... He could make it a very long afternoon Sunday.

Manny Fernandez
Miami defensive tackle,
on Minnesota
quarterback
Fran Tarkenton

SIDELINE

Before becoming an NFL coach, Bud Grant was a forward with the Minneapolis Lakers of the NBA, a receiver with the Philadelphia Eagles of the NFL and a receiver with Winnipeg of the Canadian Football League.

The crew of Skylab 3– Alan Bean, Jack Lousma and Owen Garriot– watched Super Bowl VIII from Earth orbit during their mission.

3 0   3 5   4 0   4 5

Super Bowl VIII

What can you say about Minnesota? I just recently had the helmet of Roy Winston removed from my backbone.

Larry Csonka
Miami running back on a previous meeting with the Minnesota linebacker

I get very uptight about that name. I'm not purple and I don't eat people.

Alan Page
Minnesota defensive tackle on the "Purple People Eaters" tag given the Vikings' defensive line

In a game he was like a real general in a real war. Distant. Didn't talk to anyone on the sidelines, except maybe Shula.

Nick Buoniconti
Miami linebacker on Miami quarterback Bob Griese

It's not the collision that gets you. It's what happens after you tackle him. His legs are so strong he keeps moving. He carries you. He's a movable weight.

Jeff Siemon
Minnesota linebacker describing Miami running back Larry Csonka

The Tuesday Rule .... the Tuesday Rule .... I've mellowed quite a bit. That's gotten down to a Saturday night rule for me.

Don Shula
Miami head coach, on whether he would be asking players to remain celibate from Tuesday night until after the Sunday game

40   35   30   25

Attendance	71,882
Top Ticket Price	$15
TV Average Share	73

We got to the line and Griese forgot the snap count. He turned to me, and I drew a blank. I turned to Kiick and he said it was either one or two. So I told Griese two. It was one. Griese was laughing when he handed the ball off, but he didn't see that linebacker coming at him.

Larry Csonka
Miami running back, referring to quarterback Bob Griese and running back Jim Kiick

It was a cheap shot, but an honest cheap shot. He came right at me and threw an elbow right through my mask. I could see the game meant something to him.

Larry Csonka
Miami running back, explaining a black eye and swollen nose without identifying his assailant

Miami is the best team I have ever played against and that includes the Packers of 1966 and 1967.

Carl Eller
Minnesota defensive end

After you lose in a Super Bowl, you lay behind a log, put a rag in your mouth and wait for another chance.

Bud Grant
Minnesota head coach

END ZONE

Fran Tarkenton holds the NFL records for passes attempted (6,467) and passes completed (3,686). Dan Fouts of the San Diego Chargers is next with 5,604 attempts and 3,297 completions.

In the offseason after Super Bowl VIII the goal posts were moved from the goal line to their present position at the back of the end zone.

TIME OUT
Ticket Distribution

Tickets to the Super Bowl are distributed as shown:

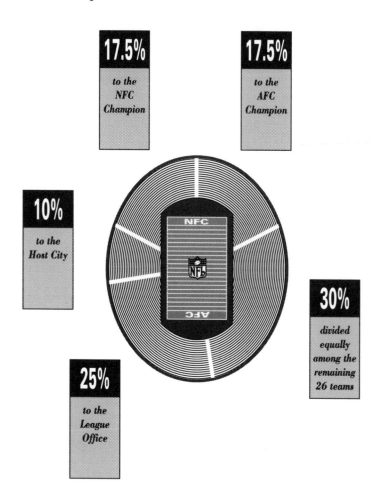

17.5%
to the NFC Champion

17.5%
to the AFC Champion

10%
to the Host City

30%
divided equally among the remaining 26 teams

25%
to the League Office

TIME OUT
National Anthem Performers

SUPER BOWL	PERFORMER(S)
I	Al Hirt (trumpeter)
II	Grambling University Band
III	Anita Bryant
IV	Al Hirt and Doc Severinsen (trumpeters)—*actor Pat O'Brien was scheduled to recite the words but his microphone was never turned on.*
V	Marvin Gaye
VI	Air Force Academy Chorale
VII	Holy Angels School Choir (Chicago)
VIII	Charlie Pride
IX	Grambling University Band
X	Tom Sullivan
XI	Vicki Carr ("America the Beautiful")
XII	Phyllis Kelly (college student)
XIII	Colgate University Band
XIV	Cheryl Ladd (actress)
XV	Helen O'Connell
XVI	Diana Ross
XVII	Leslie Easterbrook (actress)
XVIII	Barry Manilow
XIX	San Francisco Bay Area Children's Choir
XX	Wynton Marsalis (trumpeter)
XXI	Neil Diamond
XXII	Herb Alpert (trumpeter)
XXIII	Billy Joel
XXIV	Aaron Neville
XXV	Whitney Houston

Super Bowl IX

GAME SUMMARY

January 12, 1975
Tulane Stadium
New Orleans, Louisiana

The only first-half score was an end zone tackle of Vikings quarterback Fran Tarkenton by Steelers defensive end Dwight White. Minnesota's Bill Brown fumbled the second-half kickoff and Pittsburgh converted it into a touchdown by game MVP Franco Harris. The Vikings' only points were scored on Terry Brown's end zone recovery of a blocked punt.

I spoke to her last night in Detroit. The game is as good as won. I have the utmost confidence in my teammates, but you know Coach Noll's motto is, 'Whatever it takes' and if a little voodoo helps, well, why not?

John Fuqua
Pittsburgh running back, on his visit to a mystic

We heard that so often we always said he had it embroidered on his shorts.

Ray Mansfield
Pittsburgh center on Noll's use of the phrase 'Whatever it takes'

What we plan to do is put up our Steel Curtain and stop everything they do.

(Mean) Joe Greene
Pittsburgh defensive tackle

	1	2	3	4	
Pittsburgh Steelers	0	2	7	7	**16**
Minnesota Vikings	0	0	0	6	**6**

Head Coaches Chuck Noll, Bud Grant

MVP Franco Harris *Pittsburgh running back*

---

*O*ur present team isn't as good as our first Super Bowl team that lost to Kansas City.

Alan Page
Minnesota defensive tackle

*I*t will be a defensive battle. If it goes into overtime, they may play a week.

John Madden
Oakland Raiders head coach

I leave the predicting to the experts. I think we were something like 16-point favorites in our first Super Bowl game and we really blew that one.

Bud Grant
Minnesota head coach, on being a 3-point underdog

Fran Tarkenton is a lot like a guy who walks up to the roulette table and will bet on red and black …. then, just to let you know he is still there he'll throw one up on double zero. He really doesn't care if it comes up double zero or not …. he's made his point.

Andy Russell
Pittsburgh linebacker

SIDELINE

Terry Bradshaw, from Louisiana Tech, was the first player selected in the January, 1970 draft.

Minnesota quarterback Fran Tarkenton spent $3,000 on a dinner for his offensive linemen at Antoine's in the French Quarter a few days before the game.

Super Bowl IX

With two defeats the Vikings are the losingest team in the big game's brief history. But take heart, Minnesota fans .... The Pittsburgh Steelers are the NFL's losingest team over the last 40 years.

Joe Marshall
Sports Illustrated

I can't understand why guys complain about the press. For ten years, nobody ever knew who I was.

Ray Mansfield
Pittsburgh center

If we lose it's because I'm dumb. If we win it's because everyone played well and I got caught up in the action .... People are funny. If you talk slow you're dumb. If you talk fast, you're a sharpie .... Even when I play well I'm a dumbbell.

Terry Bradshaw
Pittsburgh quarterback

Even in my wildest dreams I didn't think I'd get as big a charge out of winning the Super Bowl as I have .... I love it man, I really do. I feel so good I'm almost weak.

(Mean) Joe Greene
Pittsburgh defensive tackle

4 0   3 5   3 0   2 5

Attendance	80,997
Top Ticket Price	$20
TV Average Share	72

I've looked at all sides–being a hero and being a jerk. I think I can handle this very well.

Terry Bradshaw
Pittsburgh quarterback, after the game

I'm going to cry. I keep thinking they'll win the big one. But they don't. It's going to be another long, cold winter.

Lorna Terway
St. Paul, Minnesota, on the Vikings' third Super Bowl defeat

I am not ashamed to admit that I had tears of joy in my eyes when I presented the trophy to Art Rooney that day. No man ever deserved it more.

Pete Rozelle
NFL Commissioner

Minnesota quarterback Fran Tarkenton and his teammates dumped a bucket of water off a balcony onto commentator Howard Cosell's head, which washed his toupee off.

*I*t means you're number one, and that's what it's all about.

Franco Harris
Pittsburgh running back on winning the Super Bowl

*C*an you imagine what it's like in Pittsburgh tonight? The place must be in ashes.

Jack Ham
Pittsburgh linebacker

*T*his is the biggest win of my life.

Art Rooney, Sr.
Pittsburgh owner

Pittsburgh head coach Chuck Noll allowed his players to sleep with their wives on the eve of the game, a decision Joe Greene described as "an act of faith."

Super Bowl X

GAME SUMMARY

January 18, 1976
Orange Bowl
Miami, Florida

Terry Bradshaw and Roger Staubach each threw two touchdown passes. Pittsburgh's 21-point total was scored with two touchdowns, one extra point, two field goals by Roy Gerela and a safety by Reggie Harrison. A Glen Edwards interception in the end zone was the game's last play. MVP Lynn Swann set a Super Bowl record, since broken, with 161 receiving yards on 4 catches.

I'll betcha the Cowboys jump right into the ocean once they finish practice. I hope a shark bites off Roger Staubach's legs so he can't run.

Jack Lambert
Pittsburgh linebacker, referring to Dallas' oceanfront hotel accommodations

I hate this place .... People come here to play golf and die.

Ernie (Fats) Holmes
Pittsburgh defensive tackle on Miami

I don't care for the man. He makes more money than I do, and he don't have no teeth.

Thomas (Hollywood) Henderson
Dallas linebacker, on Pittsburgh linebacker Jack Lambert

10   15   20

Pittsburgh Steelers	7	0	0	14	**21**
Dallas Cowboys	7	3	0	7	**17**

Head Coaches Chuck Noll, Tom Landry

MVP Lynn Swann *Pittsburgh wide receiver*

A "gadget" team.

The Steelers on the Cowboys

Thugs.

The Cowboys on the Steelers

If Jesus were alive today, He would be at the Super Bowl.

Norman Vincent Peale

Nothing there but gristle and meanness. No fat and he's got no brakes. Just keeps movin' till somebody puts a spoke in his wheels.

Cliff Harris

Dallas free safety, describing Pittsburgh running back Franco Harris

When I was playing for Baltimore and Pittsburgh, the quarterback's call in the huddle was a sentence long. Here it's a paragraph.

Preston Pearson

Dallas running back

SIDELINE

Dan (Bad Rad) Radakovich, Pittsburgh offensive line coach, was known for his intensity. Once, he rushed home to study the playbook, grabbed a can of beer from the refrigerator and settled down at the kitchen table. A woman he didn't recognize came in, greeted him, and informed him that his house was a block away.

In 1990 a full set of Super Bowl programs sold for $3,000.

Super Bowl X

At halftime Bradshaw and I will have an I.Q. test, but I get to pick the questions.

Roger Staubach

Dallas quarterback, referring to Pittsburgh quarterback Terry Bradshaw

Listen, I know all about the Super Bowl .... I've seen every Super Bowl that was ever played. I sat right there in front of a TV set and never moved. Now I'm in one. It's no big deal for me.

Thomas (Hollywood) Henderson

Dallas linebacker

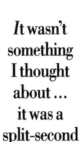

It wasn't something I thought about ... it was a split-second thing.

Jack Lambert

Pittsburgh linebacker, on throwing Dallas safety Cliff Harris to the ground after Harris tapped Pittsburgh placekicker Roy Gerela on the helmet when Gerela missed a field goal

I can't recall ever having a worse week of practice when it came to catching the ball.

Lynn Swann

Pittsburgh wide receiver and game MVP

Lynn Swann was an idol .... I'll never forget the one versus Dallas. It was the greatest catch I've ever seen.

Jerry Rice

San Francisco wide receiver, after Rice was named game MVP in Super Bowl XXIII

Attendance	80,187
Top Ticket Price	$20
TV Average Share	78

I still don't know what happened, but it split my tongue down the middle.

Reggie Harrison
Pittsburgh running back on a Dallas punt he blocked with his face

---

We're Number 1 two times .... we have championship blood in us.

Franco Harris
Pittsburgh running back

*T*he really unfortunate thing is that that team of asses is the world champions.

Jean Fugett
Dallas tight end

It has a little button on the side. Push it and the top flips up. Inside is a miniature tape recorder. Listen ... you can hear Tom Landry crying.

Chuck Noll
Pittsburgh head coach, describing his Super Bowl ring

END ZONE

In the fourth quarter, a woman left the stands and ran into the Dallas huddle, trying to give Dallas tackle Rayfield Wright a silver horseshoe good-luck charm. He refused to accept it.

Crowd scenes from the movie Black Sunday *were filmed at game X. The movie was about Arab terrorists threatening to bomb the stadium from a blimp. Fifteen years later, the Goodyear Blimp would be banned from game XXV because of the threat of terrorism connected with the Persian Gulf War.*

15   10   5

Perfecto 17-0-0

Super Bowl rings have
special powers...

Super Bowl XI

GAME SUMMARY

January 9, 1977
Rose Bowl
Pasadena, California

Oakland scored on three successive second quarter possessions to take a 16-0 halftime lead. Oakland cornerback Willie Brown returned an interception 75 yards for a touchdown, and running back Pete Banaszak scored two touchdowns.

Wife, mother, girl friend, favorite grade school teacher, whatever. That's it.

John Madden
Oakland head coach, detailing his limit of one Super Bowl guest per player

The Vikings wear elegant purple .... Oakland wears pollution. Black and gray.

Dan Jenkins
Sports Illustrated

Like clockwork, just before warmups, Fred [Biletnikoff] would be in the bathroom, heaving.

John Madden
Oakland head coach, on the MVP of game XI

| Oakland Raiders | 0 | 16 | 3 | 13 | **32** |
| Minnesota Vikings | 0 | 0 | 7 | 7 | **14** |

| Head Coaches | John Madden, Bud Grant |
| MVP | Fred Biletnikoff *Oakland wide receiver* |

*B*oth teams had been called choke artists before the game. After there would be only one choker left.

Dan Jenkins
Sports Illustrated

This team is literally on fire to play this game.

Fran Tarkenton
Minnesota quarterback

I get up with nightmares after seeing Alan run by me in my dreams.

Gene Upshaw
Oakland guard, on having to block Minnesota defensive tackle Alan Page

When you're as big as I am you like to hang around close to the ground.

John Madden
Oakland head coach, at 250+ pounds, on his fear of flying

*O*tis Sistrunk is from the University of Mars.

Alex Karras
on Oakland's bald-headed defensive lineman

Nothing can stop us now.

Carl Eller
Minnesota defensive end after the Vikings' NFC championship victory

SIDELINE

The winner of the AFC Championship Game gets the Lamar Hunt Trophy, named for the AFL founder and owner of the Kansas City Chiefs.

The George Halas Trophy goes to the NFC Champion. It was named for the late NFL player, coach, and owner of the Chicago Bears.

30   35   40   45

Super Bowl XI

We are lucky to get out of here with our lives.

Brent McClanahan
Minnesota running back

We just played them on the wrong day. Next time we'll play them on Wednesday.

Bud Grant
Minnesota head coach

When you lose like this, you want to go hide …. Right now, I can't imagine getting up tomorrow or playing next year.

Fran Tarkenton
Minnesota quarterback

We're going to run through the entire AFC to see if there's anybody we can beat. So far, we've turned Kansas City, Miami, Pittsburgh, and Oakland into dynasties.

Fran Tarkenton
Minnesota quarterback

A stick of gum would have been enough.

Fred Biletnikoff
Oakland wide receiver and game MVP, clutching his MVP award

Attendance	103,438		
Top Ticket Price	$20		
TV Average Share	73		

This loss is as frustrating as the first one, the second one and the third. We'll win it yet.

Carl Eller
Minnesota defensive end

I don't take anything away from the Vikings. We played a great football team that day.

Art Shell
Oakland offensive lineman

Why? Who the hell knows?

Mick Tingelhoff
Minnesota center, when asked, after he had retired, to name a reason for the Vikings' four Super Bowl losses

At least we were there, doggone it. A lot of other teams would love to have been in a Super Bowl.

Paul Krause
Minnesota free safety

You could say that we've made more money in the Super Bowl than most teams.

Bud Grant
Minnesota head coach

END ZONE

Art Shell and Gene Upshaw, Oakland offensive linemen and future Hall-of-Famers, dominated their side of the line, keeping Minnesota defensive end Jim Marshall from making any quarterback sacks, tackles or assists on tackles.

Bud Grant, Vikings head coach, took 4 teams to the Super Bowl but never won.

Super Bowl XII

GAME SUMMARY

January 15, 1978
Louisiana Superdome
New Orleans, Louisiana

Dallas' "Doomsday II Defense" forced 8 Denver turnovers. The Broncos' "Orange Crush" defense had little effect on the Cowboys' offense, which featured two exciting touchdown plays: Roger Staubach's 45-yard pass to Butch Johnson and running back Robert Newhouse's 29-yard pass to Golden Richards.

Dallas is like their coach. They are about as emotional as a Swiss bank.

Jim Murray
Los Angeles Times

He's a perfectionist. If he was married to Raquel Welch, he'd expect her to cook.

Don Meredith
former Dallas
quarterback on head
coach Tom Landry

The Cowboys are like a woman who's had a lot of facelifts. They're a fantasy from their uniforms to their stadium, which is like being in a living room.

Howie Long
Oakland Raiders
defensive lineman,
remembering the
Dallas team

| Dallas Cowboys | 10 | 3 | 7 | 7 | **27** |
| Denver Broncos | 0 | 0 | 10 | 0 | **10** |

Head Coaches	Tom Landry, Red Miller
MVP	Randy White, Harvey Martin
	defensive linemen

I didn't even know who was playin' until I got here .... I'm here because I hear the Super Bowl is the biggest party in the world.

Billy Carter
brother of U.S. President Jimmy Carter

*M*an, the Cowboys are all business. I like it like that. The Orange Crush is Orange Mush.

Tony Dorsett
Dallas running back

*O*range Crush is soda water, baby. You drink it. It don't win football games.

Harvey Martin
Dallas defensive end

At one point in the first half, Robert Newhouse got hold of my arm and said, 'Roger, you've got to get hold of this team.' I told him, 'Robert, I'm trying to get hold of myself.' Eventually, we did.

Roger Staubach
Dallas quarterback referring to his running back teammate

SIDELINE

Roger Staubach's five Super Bowl fumbles are a career record.

The winners' and losers' shares increased for the first time since the Super Bowl began. Each member of the winning team received $18,000 and each member of the losing team received $9,000, exactly half of what the teams in Super Bowls XVII-XXV would receive.

30   35   40   45

Super Bowl XII

No more turnovers.

Offense break the ice.

Defense keep working.

Attack, attack, attack!

Halftime messages on the Broncos' locker room blackboard

They fought like a bunch of alley cats.

Red Miller
Denver head coach describing his team

We did just about everything wrong there was to do wrong.

Craig Morton
Denver quarterback

I was embarrassed.

Lyle Alzado
Denver defensive end

I'm sorry they took Morton out. I wanted him to throw me a couple.

Thomas (Hollywood) Henderson

Dallas linebacker, on Denver quarterback Craig Morton, who threw four first-half interceptions

People only remember winners, and when they think of Craig Morton, they think of him as the

(continued)

---

quarterback who lost in those Super Bowl games. They don't think about the phenomenal seasons he had just getting his teams to those games. Watching what happened to him in [Super Bowl] XII was one of the saddest things I can remember in football.

Roger Staubach
Dallas quarterback, remembering his opponent

Attendance	75,583
Top Ticket Price	$30
TV Average Share	67

These guys made more mistakes than the boss at the office Christmas party .... If Denver ever gets in the Super Bowl again, they better put handles on the football.

Jim Murray
Los Angeles Times

We felt we were a team of destiny. We felt God had a plan for us today. But maybe it was a plan for us to lose.

Jim Turner
Denver placekicker

You'll be back. Just hope it's the Minnesota Vikings you find there the next time.

Dan Jenkins
Sports Illustrated, to the Denver Broncos

It may sound corny, but it was like Rocky. We didn't win. We didn't beat the champ, but inside we feel like winners. They're making a sequel, aren't they?

Joe Rizzo
Denver linebacker

END ZONE

Super Bowl XII was the first played in a totally enclosed stadium, of which Chicago Bears head coach Mike Ditka would say, "[Indoor domes] weren't meant for football .... Domes should be used for roller rinks."

Dallas right defensive tackle Randy White was nicknamed "Manster"– half man and half monster.

Super Bowl XIII

GAME SUMMARY

January 21, 1979
Orange Bowl
Miami, Florida

In the first Super Bowl rematch, Dallas scored with 2 first-half touchdowns– a 39-yard pass from Roger Staubach to Tony Hill and a 37-yard fumble return by linebacker Mike Hegman.

In the second half, the Steelers scored 2 touchdowns in 19 seconds.

Dallas responded with 2 touchdowns, one following an onside kick. A second onside kick failed and the Steelers ran out the clock.

MVP Terry Bradshaw threw 4 touchdown passes.

I'll either be at the White House or at Camp David watching the game. I have a $5 bet with Miss Lillian. I'm for the Dallas Cowboys and Miss Lillian is rooting for the Pittsburgh Steelers.

Jimmy Carter
President of the United States, referring to his mother Lillian Carter

I don't think I'll watch it. I'll be out skiing. The Super Bowl is a lot of sound and fury signifying nothing.

Robert Redford
Actor

Pittsburgh Steelers	7	14	0	14	**35**
Dallas Cowboys	7	7	3	14	**31**

Head Coaches	Chuck Noll, Tom Landry
MVP	Terry Bradshaw *Pittsburgh quarterback*

I root against Dallas by instinct. The Dallas team does not seem to have much fun when they play. Pittsburgh looks like it's having a lot of fun. I think Tom Landry is the first successful example of cybernetics, someone brought back from another life.

Morley Safer
Television broadcaster

The rough, rugged basic Steelers … the clean, cosmopolitan, finesse Cowboys. The guys in the ties and dark suits against the guys in the hardhats and rolled-up sleeves. That contrast … that was the thing between us.

Cliff Harris
Dallas free safety

*I'*m the greatest linebacker who ever played football. Hey, Dick Butkus was just a lineman standing on two legs.

Thomas (Hollywood) Henderson
Dallas linebacker, referring to the former Chicago Bears middle linebacker and Hall-of-Famer

SIDELINE

Seven players hold the record of playing in 5 Super Bowls: Larry Cole, Cliff Harris, D.D. Lewis, Preston Pearson, Charlie Waters, Rayfield Wright and Marv Fleming.

In the offseason prior to 1978, a rule change made it illegal to have defensive contact with receivers five yards beyond the line of scrimmage. It was known as the 'Mel Blount Rule' because of the Pittsburgh cornerback's tendency to leave receivers half-conscious, and it raised the premium on the passing game.

Super Bowl XIII

I put a lot of pressure on myself to see if I can play up to my mouth.

Thomas (Hollywood) Henderson
Dallas linebacker

*E*mpty barrels make the most noise.

Chuck Noll
Pittsburgh head coach, on Thomas Henderson's boasts

I'm doing everybody a favor. I'm getting some people to hate me. I'm getting some people to love me. I'm getting some excitement going around here.

Thomas (Hollywood) Henderson
Dallas linebacker, on why he talked so much

*B*less his heart, he's got to be the sickest man in America.

Verne Lundquist
Television commentator, on Dallas tight end Jackie Smith who, all by himself in the end zone, dropped a pass

*W*hen I saw the flag, I was mad, damn right. It was the closest I'll ever come to punching an official, I guess.

Benny Barnes
Dallas cornerback, on an interference call that set up a Pittsburgh touchdown

*T*he kiss of death.

Tom Landry
Dallas head coach, describing the same call which cost field judge Fred Swearingen his job two years later

40   35   30   25

Attendance	79,484
Top Ticket Price	$30
TV Average Share	74

Our guys started celebrating when it was 35-17, and it made me mad.

Terry Bradshaw
Pittsburgh quarterback

Terry Bradshaw couldn't spell 'cat' if you spotted him the 'c' and the 'a.'

Thomas (Hollywood) Henderson
Dallas linebacker

Go ask Thomas Henderson if I was dumb.

Terry Bradshaw
Pittsburgh quarterback, after the Steelers' victory

I rated his intelligence. I didn't rate his ability.

Thomas (Hollywood) Henderson
Dallas linebacker, on his earlier comments regarding Terry Bradshaw

I set my alarm for Tuesday. I'm going to party.

Rick Moser
Pittsburgh rookie running back, after the game

END ZONE

George Halas holds the NFL record for career victories by a head coach with 325. At the beginning of the 1991 season Don Shula was next with 298. Only 17 others have over 100 career victories, including current head coaches Chuck Noll (202), Chuck Knox (171), and Joe Gibbs (113).

The ultimate good luck charm for a Pittsburgh fan was a "Terrible Towel." The black and gold hand towel, to be waved at games, was the brainstorm of Pittsburgh sportscaster Myron Cope.

15   10   5

Super Bowl Logos On Parade

**First World
Championship
Game AFL vs NFL**

SUPER BOWL VIII

SUPER BOWL II

SUPER BOWL
IX

SUPER
BOWL III

SUPER
BOWL X

SUPER
BOWL IV

SUPER BOWL XI

SUPER BOWL V

SUPER BOWL
XII

SUPER BOWL VI

SUPER BOWL VII

SUPER BOWL
XIII

Super Bowl XIV

GAME SUMMARY

January 20, 1980
Rose Bowl
Pasadena, California

The Rams, who had posted a 9-7 regular season record, led at halftime 13-10. The Steelers came from behind twice in the second half on touchdown passes to wide receivers Lynn Swann and John Stallworth. Pittsburgh defensive back Larry Anderson returned 5 kickoffs for 162 yards. Terry Bradshaw won his second consecutive MVP award before a record-setting crowd.

Sure it is, it comes in a bigger box.

Fred Dryer
Los Angeles defensive end, when asked if the Super Bowl was bigger than death

There are ways to make Super Bowl XIV more competitive. Put weights on the Steelers. Make Terry Bradshaw throw left-handed. Let the Rams play with twelve men. Then it might be a game.

Bob Rubin
Sportswriter
Miami Herald

10   15   20

Pittsburgh Steelers	3	7	7	14	**31**
Los Angeles Rams	7	6	6	0	**19**

Head Coaches	Chuck Noll, Ray Malavasi
MVP	Terry Bradshaw *Pittsburgh quarterback*

I'd like to see the Super Bowl a little more like a wrestling promotion .... bring in some Arabian guards with swords to surround the field and put Howard Cosell up in a big throne. Make him wear a fez thirty feet tall.

Fred Dryer
Los Angeles defensive end

I think [Ferragamo] will get scared to death. I know I went through it.

Terry Bradshaw
Pittsburgh quarterback on the Los Angeles quarterback's first (and only) trip to the Super Bowl

60-Prevent-Slot-Hook-And-Go

Terry Bradshaw
Pittsburgh quarterback, calling what was to become a 73-yard touchdown pass to John Stallworth that gave the Steelers a 24-19 lead

I never liked that play. Neither did Bradshaw .... When we tried it in practice, it never worked.

John Stallworth
Pittsburgh receiver describing 60-Prevent-Slot-Hook-And-Go

SIDELINE

Football sequences for the film Heaven Can Wait were filmed at Super Bowl XIV. Los Angeles quarterback Vince Ferragamo was Warren Beatty's stand-in.

A reported link between the Super Bowl and stock market activity went like this: if a team from the old AFL wins, the market will go down for the rest of the year. If a team from the old NFL wins, the market will go up. After game XIV the prediction was true 13 of 14 years, judging by Standard & Poor's 500 Index.

Super Bowl XIV

Cliff Stoudt has two Super Bowl rings from the Pittsburgh Steelers for doing nothing more strenuous than standing on the sideline keeping Terry Bradshaw's toupee dry.

Tony Kornheiser
Washington Post

Just once I'd like to wake up sore on Monday morning.

Cliff Stoudt
Pittsburgh third-string quarterback, on not playing once in his three-year career

Jack Lambert hollered so hard in the huddle that I got scared. I can't say what he said, but he got real red in the face.

Donnie Shell
Pittsburgh strong safety on his linebacker teammate

It was like when you got in a fight when you were a kid and you were getting beat up and your big brother came along.

Ray Mansfield
Pittsburgh center on linebacker Jack Lambert's ability to fire up his teammates

The Steelers are like the great Yankee teams used to be. The peer pressure is very strong. Just putting on the uniform motivates a player to perform beyond his potential.

Art Rooney, Jr.
Pittsburgh administrator

40 35 30 25

Attendance	103,985
Top Ticket Price	$30
TV Average Share	67

The thing everybody knew about the Hollywood Rams was that you could beat them in the fourth quarter.

Eddie Brown

Los Angeles wide receiver (the Rams led 19-17 after three quarters and were outscored 14-0 in the fourth quarter)

They did not outplay us. We ran on them. We threw on them. But we just didn't get the big plays. I'm sure we'll be back in the Super Bowl next year.

Ray Malavasi

Los Angeles head coach (the Rams have not returned to the Super Bowl)

Waiting for the Rams to win a Super Bowl is like leaving the porch light on for Jimmy Hoffa.

Milton Berle
Comedian

15   10   5

Super Bowl XV

GAME SUMMARY

January 25, 1981
Louisiana Superdome
New Orleans, Louisiana

With 9 seconds left in the first quarter, MVP Jim Plunkett completed an 80-yard touchdown pass to running back Kenny King. Oakland linebacker Rod Martin intercepted 3 passes as the Eagles stayed away from Raiders' linebacker Ted Hendricks. Oakland became the first wild-card team to win the Super Bowl.

'What the hell's a woman doing on the field?'

Mrs. Marie Lombardi

when asked what her late husband, Vince Lombardi, would have said about her performing the coin toss before the game

THE BEST WAY TO KILL TIME IS TO WORK IT TO DEATH.

Sign in the Philadelphia locker room, hung there by head coach Dick Vermeil

---

The main thing is to be a force, so guys will say, 'Tooz is kicking butts.'

John Matuszak
Oakland defensive end, on his personal goals for the game

My bomb scare is Plunkett.

Dick Vermeil
Philadelphia head coach, on rumors that his team had experienced a bomb threat

Oakland Raiders	14	0	10	3	**27**
Philadelphia Eagles	0	3	0	7	**10**

Head Coaches Tom Flores, Dick Vermeil
MVP Jim Plunkett *Oakland quarterback*

I'd ship his butt home.

Dick Vermeil
Philadelphia head coach commenting on what he would do if he caught a player breaking curfew

If Tom Flores sent home every guy on this football team who screwed up, he'd be the only guy on the sideline.

Gene Upshaw
Oakland guard

Three a.m.? Was that all it was? … I am the enforcer. That's why I was out on the streets— to make sure no one else was.

John Matuszak
Oakland defensive end, on New Orleans' nightlife

I don't know. Ask Jimmy the Greek.

Dick Vermeil
Philadelphia head coach, when asked why the Eagles were 3-point favorites

We have an image of being renegades and bad guys. We wear black and that is associated with the villains …. But we're really not that bad. They're pretty nice guys once you get to know them.

Tom Flores
Oakland head coach, on his players

SIDELINE

Super Bowl XV came about a week after the release of American hostages from Iran. The Superdome was wrapped with a huge yellow ribbon and fans sang "Tie a Yellow Ribbon." Players wore yellow tape on their helmets.

Tom Flores, Oakland head coach, was the first Super Bowl player to be the head coach of a Super Bowl team. This feat was later duplicated by Forrest Gregg, Mike Ditka, Dan Reeves and Sam Wyche.

Super Bowl XV

They've got this big reputation as intimidators, but I think that died when Jack Tatum and George Atkinson left.

Ron Jaworski
Philadelphia quarterback, on the Oakland defense

His chances of catching any balls on my side are very slim. If the Eagles throw a lot to my side, I might catch more balls than Carmichael. That is not a challenge. That is a fact.

Lester Hayes
Oakland cornerback, on Philadelphia All-Pro tight end Harold Carmichael

The motto of our team is 'Pride and Poise.' Jim Plunkett represents the best of both.

Gene Upshaw
Oakland guard

[The Eagles] weren't ready for what we gave them today. They were over-confident, and [their coach] got them that way. He didn't let them go out all week. You can't treat a man like a boy and expect him to play like a man.

John Matuszak
Oakland defensive end, on why the Eagles seemed to lack intensity

4 0   3 5   3 0   2 5

Attendance	76,135
Top Ticket Price	$40
TV Average Share	63

I always had confidence that we would do it .... Now everyone is asking what it will be like on Sunday when suddenly ... people all across the country will be talking about me .... How should I know? I won't hear them.

Ron Jaworski
Philadelphia quarterback

Anyone who says one loss cannot ruin a season never lost a Super Bowl.

Dick Vermeil
Philadelphia head coach

This is without a doubt our finest hour.

Al Davis
Oakland managing general partner

I thought the media over-dramatized my story. Everything I read that week had the same theme: 'Plunkett resurrected ... Plunkett back from the scrap heap.' I never thought I was that far gone.

Jim Plunkett
Oakland quarterback and game MVP

END ZONE

The Raiders had 11 Super Bowl veterans, including guard Gene Upshaw, the only man to play in Super Bowls in three different decades (games II, XI and XV).

Eleanor Dienstag of New York City threw "A Women's Party: An Alternative to the Super Bowl" for 40 of her friends during game XV. "It's not an act of hostility .... It's just that I always found Super Bowl Sunday ... dreary and boring."

15   10   5

We are lucky
to get out of here
with our lives.

Doink!

Wap!

Super Bowl XVI

GAME SUMMARY

January 24, 1982
Pontiac Silverdome
Pontiac, Michigan

San Francisco took a 20-0 halftime lead on 2 field goals by Ray Wersching and 2 touchdowns. Between 2 second-half Cincinnati touchdowns, the 49ers made a spirited goal-line stand denying four Bengal attempts from the 3-yard line. Game MVP Joe Montana completed 14 of 22 passes for 157 yards.

I've got the game on the radio. We're leading 7-0. The trainer is calling the plays.

Bill Walsh
San Francisco head coach, joking to half the 49ers team while they were delayed in traffic on the way to the Silverdome (They arrived at 2:50 for 3:00 warmups. Vice President George Bush's motorcade had blocked traffic.)

Chico Norton, our equipment manager, volunteered to play quarterback.

Randy Cross
San Francisco guard, continuing the joke

You feel like you're in a living room.

Isaac Curtis
Cincinnati wide receiver, on playing in the Silverdome in Pontiac, Michigan

San Francisco 49ers	7	13	6	0	**26**
Cincinnati Bengals	0	0	7	14	**21**

Head Coaches Bill Walsh, Forrest Gregg
MVP Joe Montana *San Francisco quarterback*

Ed Jones: You just beat America's team.

Joe Montana: And you can watch us in the Super Bowl just like everyone else in America.

Exchange between Ed (Too Tall) Jones, Dallas Cowboy defensive end and Joe Montana, San Francisco quarterback, after the 49ers beat the Cowboys in the 1981 NFC Championship Game

Things have been hectic since that catch. I can't even count how many interviews I've done. It was tough on Shawn [his fiance]. She said I wouldn't talk with her because she didn't have a microphone.

Dwight Clark
San Francisco wide receiver, on reactions to his game-winning reception in the NFC Championship Game

Bill would probably just start all over again and find things that worked in high school or junior high.

Joe Montana
San Francisco quarterback, when asked if he ever worried about his head coach Bill Walsh running out of new tricks

Basically, I'm scared to death.

Bill Walsh
San Francisco head coach, describing how he felt before the Super Bowl

SIDELINE

Joe Montana finished his first full season as a starter with a win at Super Bowl XVI.

When the 49ers arrived at their hotel on Monday, a pushy bellman began grabbing the baggage. The players walked past him, shoving him away. Minutes went by before one of them recognized their head coach, Bill Walsh, who said, "You've got to have some fun sometimes."

30   35   40   45

Super Bowl XVI

I think I'm as expert as anyone coaching football today. Plus I may have an artistic ability that adds a certain flair to what I do.

Bill Walsh

San Francisco head coach, when asked, 'Are you a genius?'

You know, [Bill Walsh] believes that genius tag .... But the genius really wears number 16.

Terry Bradshaw

former Pittsburgh Steelers quarterback, referring to Joe Montana

Wright depends more on ability and speed. Lott gets up in your face and tries to manhandle you.

Cris Collinsworth

Cincinnati wide receiver, on San Francisco's rookie cornerbacks, Eric Wright and Ronnie Lott

[Critics] use the word 'finesse' when they don't understand what they're watching ...

Randy Cross

San Franciso guard replying to criticism that the 49ers played 'finesse' football to avoid a more physical game

Attendance	81,270
Top Ticket Price	$40
TV Average Share	73

It's not difficult being on the stage. Not when you enjoy attention. You put a crowd in front of me, there ain't nothin' I can't do.

Pete Johnson
Cincinnati running back

Johnson is like a Sherman Tank.

Jack (Hacksaw) Reynolds
San Francisco linebacker, describing Cincinnati running back Pete Johnson

For years, the Bengals drafted kids that looked like Tarzan, and played like Jane.

Cris Collinsworth
Cincinnati wide receiver remembering the Super Bowl XVI team

How good are we? We're the world champions aren't we?

Jack (Hacksaw) Reynolds
San Francisco linebacker

We were so young, we didn't know we weren't supposed to win.

Randy Cross
San Francisco guard

END ZONE

Half of the Cincinnati starters were either first- or second-round draft picks.

Pontiac, Michigan, was the first "cold weather" Super Bowl host city. Sub-zero windchill during Super Bowl week made wool hats with team logos a hot promotional item.

Super Bowl XVII

GAME SUMMARY

January 30, 1983
Rose Bowl
Pasadena, California

Game MVP John Riggins carried 38 times for 166 yards behind Washington's offensive line, called the "Hogs." The Redskins' defense held Miami quarterback David Woodley to 4 pass completions in 14 attempts. The Dolphins' Fulton Walker returned a kickoff 98 yards for a touchdown–a Super Bowl record. The Hogs also helped establish a record by blocking for 276 rushing yards.

The main thing I enjoy is the fact that 26 teams in the NFL are at home watching this game on television. There is a certain amount of enjoyment in that.

George Starke
Washington offensive tackle

The Super Bowl is a day of national celebration when for a few hours nearly everyone in America puts aside his everyday concerns, gathers his family and friends around the big screen TV to watch– not eat– a turkey.

Mike Littwin
Los Angeles Times

Washington Redskins	0	10	3	14	**27**
Miami Dolphins	7	10	0	0	**17**

Head Coaches Joe Gibbs, Don Shula

MVP John Riggins *Washington running back*

What does the Super Bowl mean? An opportunity to fulfill a dream. Other than that, just another football game.

John Riggins
Washington running back

We've busted our asses to get here .... Nobody can beat us as a team, and it's worth $70,000 and a big ring!

Joe Theismann
Washington quarterback to his teammates before the game

I'm speechless.

Joe Theismann
Washington quarterback, after the game

It must have been totally insulting to play defense against us, because everybody knew what we were going to do. We only had two running plays ... It was like we just said, 'Here we come ... try to stop us.'

George Starke
Washington right tackle

SIDELINE

"The Hogs" got their name when Washington offensive coordinator Joe Bugel looked at guard Russ Grimm in practice and told him he looked like a hog wallowing around in the dirt. Bugel had "Hogs" T-shirts and caps made, and the name stuck. Miami's defense was known as "The Killer Bees" because six starters had last names beginning with "B."

At halftime of game XVII, the Redskins trailed 17-10 though they had gained more yards and run more plays than the Dolphins.

Super Bowl XVII

Whoever I go against in the Super Bowl, I think I'll beat him. No, I think I'll *dominate* him.

Dexter Manley
Washington defensive end

The only thing you have to understand is that [Dexter] Manley has the I.Q. of a grapefruit.

Mike Ditka
Chicago Bears head coach

John Riggins was Mr. Universe, Mr. All-World. Their offense was no secret: 'Give it to John.'

Doug Betters
Miami defensive end on the Redskins and their star running back

The bottom line is that, despite the fancy things they tried, it was the pounding, the old fashioned stuff, that did us in.

Don Shula
Miami head coach

I don't think you would be much of an athlete if you didn't feel lousy after losing a Super Bowl game.

Bob Brudzinski
Miami linebacker

Attendance	103,667	
Top Ticket Price	$40	
TV Average Share	69	

Reporter:
How do
you account
for your
longevity?

John Riggins:
Formaldehyde.

*Exchange in the
winners' locker room
after the game*

*A genius is
someone who
has survived
for ten years
in the
National
Football
League.
People who
know me will
tell you I'm
a man of
average
intelligence.*

Joe Gibbs
Washington head coach

Now that the
season is
over, could
you move up
to Capitol
Hill and help
us with
some of the
Congressmen?

Ronald Reagan
*President of the
United States, on the
telephone to Washington
head coach Joe Gibbs
after the game*

**Ron may
be the
President,
but today
I'm the King.**

John Riggins
*Washington running
back, after talking with
President Ronald
Reagan on the
telephone*

END ZONE

*Dollar amounts
to players on
the winning and
losing teams were
increased in
Super Bowl XVII
to $36,000 and
$18,000
respectively.*

*Some of the
biggest names in
NFL history
have coached for
Washington,
including Earl
(Curly) Lambeau,
1952-53; Otto
Graham, 1966-68;
Vince Lombardi,
1969; George
Allen, 1971-77;
and current coach
Joe Gibbs, 1981-91.*

15   10   5

Super Bowl XVIII

GAME SUMMARY

January 22, 1984
Tampa Stadium
Tampa, Florida

After nearly 5 minutes of play, the Raiders' Derrick Jensen blocked a Redskins' punt and recovered it in the end zone for a touchdown.

With twelve seconds left in the first half, Washington quarterback Joe Theismann attempted a short pass from his own 5-yard line. It was intercepted by Raider Jack Squirek who scored an easy touchdown. Marcus Allen, the game MVP, gained 191 yards on 20 carries.

Just win, Baby.

Motto of Al Davis
Los Angeles managing general partner

I'd run over my mother to win it.

Russ Grimm
Washington offensive lineman

I'd run over Grimm's mother, too.

Matt Millen
Los Angeles linebacker

We knew they were the bullies of the AFC and we were the bullies of the NFC, and it was going to be one of those games that, as John Madden says, should be played on grass.

Mark May
Washington guard

Los Angeles Raiders	7	14	14	3	**38**
Washington Redskins	0	3	6	0	**9**

Head Coaches Tom Flores, Joe Gibbs
MVP Marcus Allen *Los Angeles running back*

If the Redskins are a family, then we're an orphanage.

Tom Flores
Los Angeles head coach

I just let instinct take over.

Marcus Allen
Los Angeles running back on his 74-yard touchdown run

Howie Long would be running around the locker room. Lyle Alzado would try to bite guys. Then John Matuszak would come over and yell, 'I'm sane! I'm sane!'

Matt Millen
Los Angeles linebacker, describing his teammates

If you were filming sharks feeding, this is as close as you would get .... It's like having a root canal for the players.

Joe Theismann
Washington quarterback describing reporters during media day

SIDELINE

Media sessions highlighted the contrast in the two teams' images. The Redskins' Joe Theismann changed three-piece suits between interviews while the Raiders' Lyle Alzado wore a cut-off T-shirt and threatened to rip Theismann's head off.

The Raiders are the only team to have played in Super Bowls in three decades— the 1960s, 1970s and 1980s.

30   35   40   45

Super Bowl XVIII

He was the NFL's first triple-threat media man: radio, TV, print .... He did it all. You leave a light on in the bathroom and he'd do 20 minutes to an empty shower. Never met a microphone he didn't like.

Tony Kornheiser

Washington Post describing, in 1988, Joe Theismann's next career after retiring from football

---

You look like Barry Manilow when you see your face in the reflection in the bathroom faucet.

Curt Marsh

NFL lineman describing the pop musician who sang the national anthem

---

The Redskins picked a good day to play their worst game of the season.

Bill Thost

Los Angeles firefighter and Raiders fan

They just put an old-fashioned can of whip-ass on us.

Joe Washington

Washington running back

We got our rear ends handed to us on a platter.

Joe Theismann
Washington quarterback

We dominated them. There's nothing better than feeling you can do what you want and doing it.

Tom Flores
Los Angeles head coach

Attendance	72,920
Top Ticket Price	$60
TV Average Share	71

That was a wonderful win. You've given me some problems. I've already gotten a call from Moscow. They think Marcus Allen is a new secret weapon. They insist we dismantle it.

Ronald Reagan
President of the United States, in a call to Los Angeles head coach Tom Flores after the game, referring to the Raiders running back

One of the toughest trophy presentations I had to make was to Al Davis after Super Bowl XVIII .... We had been enmeshed in a court battle over the Raiders' move to Los Angeles in 1982.

Pete Rozelle
NFL Commissioner, remembering an awkward moment after the Raiders' win

I've been an athlete for 27 years and never a champion. There's nothing left now. This is the best; this is everything.

Lyle Alzado
Los Angeles defensive end, after the game

END ZONE

In the 1983 regular season Washington running back John Riggins set an NFL record with 24 touchdowns. O.J. Simpson and Jerry Rice are next, with 23 touchdowns each.

Washington set an NFL scoring record in 1983 with 541 points, beating the second place Cowboys by 62. The Raiders beat the Redskins in game XVIII by using an attacking defensive style that would become the standard for the rest of the decade.

The Silver Anniversary

The team was chosen by national fan balloting.

HEAD COACH　　　**Vince Lombardi**　*Green Bay Packers*

OFFENSE

Quarterback　　**Joe Montana**　*San Francisco 49ers*

Running Backs　　**Franco Harris**　*Pittsburgh Steelers*
Larry Csonka　*Miami Dolphins*

Wide Receivers　　**Lynn Swann**　*Pittsburgh Steelers*
Jerry Rice　*San Francisco 49ers*

Tight End　　**Dave Casper**　*Oakland Raiders*

Tackles　　**Art Shell**　*Oakland Raiders*
Forrest Gregg　*Green Bay Packers*

Guards　　**Gene Upshaw**　*Oakland Raiders*
Jerry Kramer　*Green Bay Packers*

Center　　**Mike Webster**　*Pittsburgh Steelers*

Super Bowl Team

DEFENSE

Ends	**L.C. Greenwood** *Pittsburgh Steelers*
	Ed (Too Tall) Jones *Dallas Cowboys*
Tackles	**(Mean) Joe Greene** *Pittsburgh Steelers*
	Randy White *Dallas Cowboys*
Inside Linebackers	**Jack Lambert** *Pittsburgh Steelers*
	Mike Singletary *Chicago Bears*
Outside Linebackers	**Jack Ham** *Pittsburgh Steelers*
	Ted Hendricks *Baltimore Colts, Oakland Raiders*
Cornerbacks	**Ronnie Lott** *San Francisco 49ers*
	Mel Blount *Pittsburgh Steelers*
Safeties	**Donnie Shell** *Pittsburgh Steelers*
	Willie Wood *Green Bay Packers*

SPECIAL TEAMS

Punter	**Ray Guy** *Oakland Raiders*
Placekicker	**Jan Stenerud** *Kansas City Chiefs*
Kick Returner	**John Taylor** *San Francisco 49ers*

Super Bowl XIX

GAME SUMMARY

January 20, 1985
Stanford Stadium
Stanford, California

The teams' high-powered offenses, led by quarterbacks Joe Montana and Dan Marino, combined for a record 17 first-quarter points. The 49ers continued with 21 second-quarter points. San Francisco's Roger Craig scored 3 touchdowns and MVP Joe Montana passed for a record 331 yards.

Only in America ... and fortunately only once a year.

George Vecsey
New York Times,
on the Super Bowl

Whoever has the ball last will probably win.

Mike Ditka
Chicago Bears
head coach

The Super Bowl is a goldfish bowl .... There's no getting away, no let up.

Randy Cross
San Francisco guard

That's the price of success. I'd pay it anytime.

Fred Dean
San Francisco
defensive end

San Francisco 49ers	7	21	10	0	**38**
Miami Dolphins	10	6	0	0	**16**

Head Coaches Bill Walsh, Don Shula
MVP Joe Montana *San Francisco quarterback*

I got more ticket requests than Ticketron. I was getting calls at two in the morning from people saying, 'Remember me? I sat behind you in fourth grade. Can you get me two tickets to the game?'

Dan Bunz
San Francisco linebacker on the distractions of playing so close to home

… the home-field disadvantage.

Randy Cross
San Francisco guard's comment on playing close to home

We were 17 and 1 and people were asking us, 'Gee, do you really think you can stay with the Dolphins?' It was like a slap in the face.

Randy Cross
San Francisco guard

All week it was Miami, Miami, Miami, every time we turned around. You people were overlooking us.

Joe Montana
San Francisco quarterback to reporters after the game

SIDELINE

President Ronald Reagan did the honorary coin toss by television from the White House. It was broadcast on the huge stadium screen.

The 49ers in 1984 outscored their collective opponents 2 to 1 during the regular season—475 points to 227. 10 players were voted to the Pro Bowl, including all four starting defensive backs.

Super Bowl XIX

They talk about [Dan] Marino's lightning-quick release, how swiftly he can complete his passes. Well, we can do some of that, too, you know.

Bill Walsh
San Francisco head coach

Don Strock backed up three different Super Bowl quarterbacks for Miami. He stood right beside Don Shula for so long people thought they'd been surgically bonded.

Tony Kornheiser
Washington Post in a commentary on non-playing Super Bowl winners

[Bubba] Paris has three weaknesses: breakfast, lunch and dinner.

Ed Werder
Sportswriter commenting on the San Francisco tackle known for his considerable size

Things just sputtered for us and fell into place for them.

Mark Clayton
Miami wide receiver

We were dominated to the point where one play didn't make much of a difference.

Don Shula
Miami head coach, shrugging off a questionable call by the officials

Attendance	84,059		
Top Ticket Price	$60		
TV Average Share	63		

What happened to Clayton and Duper? What happened to them was [cornerbacks] Eric Wright and Ronnie Lott and our defensive line.

Keena Turner

San Francisco linebacker, referring to Miami wide receivers Mark Clayton and Mark Duper

If their I.Q.s were five points lower, they'd be geraniums.

Russ Francis

San Francisco tight end describing defensive linemen

All we heard about was Marino and how to stop them. Nobody said anything about how to stop us.

Joe Montana

San Francisco quarterback

*W*hen you get beat the way we got beat, you have to take your hat off to them, and that's what I'll do.

Don Shula
Miami head coach

END ZONE

In 1984, his second pro season, Dan Marino set NFL records with 5,084 passing yards, 48 touchdown passes and 362 completions.

The 1984 Dolphins were known as "Don Shula's Flying Circus" because of their ability to make games exciting and fun to watch.

15   10   5

Super Bowl XX

GAME SUMMARY

January 26, 1986
Louisiana Superdome
New Orleans, Louisiana

The Bears' league-leading defense, coached by Buddy Ryan, dominated, holding the Patriots to 7 yards rushing. William (Refrigerator) Perry, a 320-pound Chicago defensive tackle, also ran for a 1-yard touchdown. The Bears also scored on an interception return by Reggie Phillips and a safety by Henry Waechter.

Pressure's not a bad thing, if you can handle it.

Mike Ditka
Chicago head coach

Just showing them where it hurts.

Jim McMahon
Chicago quarterback, after suffering a bruised buttock and mooning a media helicopter during practice

Folk heroes come and go. Just think about Davey Crockett. I haven't heard his name mentioned all week. You're only a hero when you're doing it.

Mike Ditka
Chicago head coach on why he benched William Perry in the season following the Super Bowl

Chicago Bears	13	10	21	2	**46**
New England Patriots	3	0	0	7	**10**

Head Coaches Mike Ditka, Raymond Berry

MVP Richard Dent *Chicago defensive end*

... more dominant than the Steel Curtain.

Tom Landry
Dallas head coach comparing the Bears to the Pittsburgh Steeler's legendary defense

If you even gained yardage, they were upset.

Garin Veris
New England defensive end on the Chicago defense, which held the Patriots to -19 yards in the first half

[Ditka] reminds me of many of the coaches back in the NFL of the 1950s: fascist, loud ... but not exactly Phi Beta Kappa.

Jim Brown
Former star running back for the Cleveland Browns

Regardless of what happens tomorrow, you'll always be my heroes.

Buddy Ryan
Chicago defensive coordinator, in a Saturday night pregame speech to his squad, knowing this would be his last game with them

SIDELINE

Commissioner Pete Rozelle fined Jim McMahon for wearing a headband with a shoe company's name in a playoff game. McMahon's new headband for the NFC Championship Game said "ROZELLE."

At the time of Super Bowl XX, the Chicago Bears' video "The Super Bowl Shuffle" ranked second only to Michael Jackson's "Thriller" in videocassette sales. The rap song was a stomp- and sing-along highlight at halftime.

Super Bowl XX

The tears were streaming down his face. There were a lot of wet eyes in the room, including my own. I couldn't sleep that night just thinking about it. It was like your father telling you, 'I've got to go somewhere else, but you're still my son.'

(continued)

It was like watching your family break up.

Mike Singletary
Chicago middle linebacker, on Ryan's speech and the players' knowledge that Ryan had been offered a head coaching job with the Philadelphia Eagles and probably would be leaving the Bears

In the third quarter, I was ready to go to Bourbon Street.

Steve McMichael
Chicago defensive tackle

When you looked into [Tony] Eason's eyes, you saw the same eyes as the first time we played them this year—a little confused.

Mike Singletary
Chicago middle linebacker, on the New England quarterback

It was like trying to beat back the tide with a broom.

Ron Wooten
New England guard, on the Chicago defense

If you're in the league long enough, you're going to get your rear end handed to you, and that's what happened to us today.

Raymond Berry
New England head coach

40   35   30   25

Attendance	73,818
Top Ticket Price	$75
TV Average Share	70

Yes, I'm disappointed …. But that's the way the game goes.

Walter Payton

Chicago running back in his eleventh season, on not being given the ball to score a sure touchdown on a 1-yard run

I'm not embarrassed … I'm humiliated.

Ron Wooten
New England guard

There's a certain point where you think, 'This game's over' …. You have to keep playing, but [that feeling is] in your heart.

Garin Veris
New England defensive end

Mr. Halas' birthday would have been February 2. This is a fitting gift. Because of Mr. Halas, I am here, and I will never forget that. I think he is smiling somewhere today.

Mike Ditka
Chicago head coach, referring to George (Papa Bear) Halas, the late Bears' owner who died October 31, 1983

END ZONE

The Patriots were the first wild-card team to reach the Super Bowl by winning three playoff games on the road, beating the Jets, Raiders and Dolphins.

The Chicago Bears lead the NFL with 10 retired uniform numbers: #3 Bronko Nagurski, #5 George McAfee, #28 Willie Galimore, #34 Walter Payton, #41 Brian Piccolo, #42 Sid Luckman, #56 Bill Hewitt, #61 Bill George, #66 Bulldog Turner, and #77 Red Grange.

Just win, Baby.

YEAH!

Super Bowl XXI

GAME SUMMARY

January 25, 1987
Rose Bowl
Pasadena, California

The first half of this game ended with a 10-9 Denver lead. The Giants dominated the second half. Game MVP Phil Simms led the way, completing a record 88 percent of his passes (22 of 25) for 286 yards and 3 touchdown passes.

When you're yelling and your eyes turn red and you feel like slapping your mother, that's when you know you're ready to play ball.

Lawrence Taylor
New York linebacker

They're creative ... we're a little more traditional.

Bill Parcells
New York head coach, comparing the Giants and the Broncos

I hope the game is not one-sided. If it isn't, we have a chance to win it.

Dan Reeves
Denver head coach

We'd better win. Nobody is going to remember this if we lose.

Tony Galbreath
New York running back

New York Giants	7	2	17	13	**39**
Denver Broncos	10	0	0	10	**20**

Head Coaches Bill Parcells, Dan Reeves

MVP Phil Simms *New York quarterback*

I'm telling you guys, I feel great. I'm gonna be throwing some fastballs today. Give me time and I'll rip 'em.

Phil Simms
New York quarterback, to his offensive teammates before the game

*A*ll year long we heard that we were the weak underbellies of the team. Well we've got five tough s.o.b.'s that will go over the middle to catch the ball. We get our heads knocked off, our helmets cracked, and we get back up. I'll take that over world-class,

(continued)

pretty boy wide-outs anytime.

Phil McConkey
New York wide receiver

*B*efore the game we were anxious to get out there on the field, after this long week in California. We were like caged animals: 'Let us out! Let us out!'

Kenny Hill
New York safety

SIDELINE

During warm-ups, the public address system blasted "New York, New York" to fire up the Giants and their fans.

Halftime featured a salute to Hollywood's 100th anniversary and displayed various eras of the Hollywood cinema, from silent movies to modern musicals.

John Elway, from Stanford University, was the NFL's 1983 number one draft pick.

Super Bowl XXI

I looked up in the stands, and I saw people who wanted it as much as we did, if that's possible.

Phil McConkey
New York wide receiver

I thought, 'Uh-oh. Wear your track shoes. It could be a long day.'

Carl Banks
New York linebacker after Denver's successful opening series

[*The* Broncos] showed us no respect. I'm not taking anything away from them. But they showed us no respect throwing the ball. We were going to make them show us some today.

Phil Simms
New York quarterback

Things seem so much slower when you're on the field .... The ball seemed to be just floating down. It reminded me of when I was a kid in Buffalo catching snowflakes in my mouth.

Phil McConkey
New York wide receiver, describing his catch in the end zone

I felt the team unravel after that. I really hurt them. I'm sorry.

Rich Karlis
Denver placekicker, on his missed field goal from 34 yards out at the end of the first half

I felt I did everything I could. I gave 110 percent. That's all I could do any more.

John Elway
Denver quarterback

Attendance	101,063
Top Ticket Price	$75
TV Average Share	66

In my wildest dreams I couldn't have hoped it would work out this way.

Phil Simms
New York quarterback and game MVP

This dispelled for the last time any myth about Phil Simms. He was absolutely magnificent today.

Bill Parcells
New York head coach

Great players play great games in big games.

Lawrence Taylor
New York linebacker

As the game was going on, I didn't realize I was having that great a game .... I thought back ... Well, geez, I couldn't remember any incompletions.

Phil Simms
New York quarterback

It was the realization of something that was a long time coming. I just wish I didn't have to wait so long.

Harry Carson
New York linebacker

We buried all the ghosts tonight.

Bill Parcells
New York head coach

END ZONE

Denver's Rich Karlis followed his Super Bowl-record-tying longest field goal (48 yards) with the shortest miss (23 yards).

Jim Burt, Jr., the 5-year-old son of the New York nose tackle, was in for the ride of his life after his father got him on the sideline during the fourth quarter. At the gun, he was hoisted to his father's shoulders and taken onto the field for the victory celebration.

Super Bowl XXII

GAME SUMMARY

January 31, 1988
Jack Murphy Stadium
San Diego, California

This game featured an unprecedented scoring performance in the second quarter. The fireworks lasted just 5:47, took just 18 plays, and ended with 35 Redskins points. Washington quarterback Doug Williams threw 4 touchdown passes and rookie running back Timmy Smith rushed for 204 yards, a Super Bowl record. Doug Williams completed 18 of 29 attempts, for a Super Bowl record 340 yards, and won MVP honors.

I've been a quarterback since high school. I've always been black.

Doug Williams
Washington
quarterback, in response
to the question, "How
long have you been a
black quarterback?"

There have been times I've wanted to take a camera and mike and stick it down a throat.

Doug Williams
Washington
quarterback, on whether
some questions make
him angry

If my mama or sister are in uniform on the football field I'll do my best to run them over.

Ricky Hunley
Denver linebacker

Washington Redskins	0	35	0	7	**42**
Denver Broncos	10	0	0	0	**10**

Head Coaches	Joe Gibbs, Dan Reeves
MVP	Doug Williams *Washington quarterback*

I wouldn't do it .... Sunday's going to be a war, and they're the enemy. Why collaborate with them beforehand?

Mark May
Washington offensive tackle, on a planned joint chapel service for the Redskins and the Broncos on the night before the game

I pick the Broncos because John Elway is so versatile and so handsome. Also, the Redskins aren't psychologically committed to either quarterback. It's like a woman trying to choose between two men. She often winds up losing both.

Dr. Ruth Westheimer
Sex therapist and television talk-show host

"*Hogs*"–it's the guys with no finesse. They call us dirt bags, lunch-pail guys, blue-collar guys.

R.C. Thielemann
Washington guard, on the Redskins' offensive line, who were called the "Hogs"

We sip wine and chase women.

Motto
of "The Three Amigos"–Denver wide receivers Vance Johnson, Mark Jackson and Ricky Nattiel

SIDELINE

Some 6,000 people attended the NFL's "media" party and were served approximately 4,500 pounds of New York strip steaks, 4,500 pounds of baby-back ribs, 1,500 pounds of chicken, 2,000 Maryland crabcakes, 2,800 Maine lobsters, 500 sides of North Pacific smoked salmon, 125 gallons of fresh oyster stew, 25 bushels each of fresh mussels and clams, and 2,000 cornbread muffins.

30   35   40   45

Super Bowl XXII

[*F*ootball's] a tough game. Physically, if you don't want contact, better grab your tennis racquet.

Doug Williams
Washington quarterback

It hung there for me so pretty, just waiting to be plucked out of the sky.

Ricky Sanders
Washington wide receiver, describing a pass he caught

Sixty points wasn't out of reach. We went conservative in the second half ... because Joe Gibbs and Dan Reeves are friends.

Doug Williams
Washington quarterback

I feel very depressed. I don't want to go to work tomorrow. I don't want to work for a week.

Mike Brazelton
Denver fan

After a while our heads were spinning. It was like we were in a whirlpool, and everything was sinking.

Jim Ryan
Denver linebacker

Like a dreamland.

R.C. Thielemann
Washington guard, on the second quarter

I haven't even had a half of basketball like that.

Doug Williams
Washington quarterback, describing the second quarter

We came, we saw, we kicked their butts.

Dave Butz
Washington defensive tackle

Attendance	73,302	
Top Ticket Price	$100	
TV Average Share	62	

*H*ell, they kept talking about a black quarterback. He could have been yellow, pink or polka dot–what we saw tonight was a great quarterback.

Jack Kent Cooke
Washington owner, on Redskins quarterback Doug Williams

*R*edskin, black skin ... it all rhymes with win.

Doug Williams
Washington quarterback

You'll hear a lot of calls for Joe Gibbs to run for President.

Jim Berry
Washington, D.C., sportscaster

[Some Redskins fans] wore hog noses .... My staff told me that wouldn't be very presidential.

Ronald Reagan
President of the United States, describing the scene at a White House reception for the Redskins

*W*ashington Has a New Mr. Smith

Washington Post headline
referring to Washington rookie running back Timmy Smith's 204 rushing yards effort

*M*y bank account is 47 cents. But who needs a job when you win the Super Bowl?

Tim Rader
Washington fan

END ZONE

Coaches and a dozen players held a joint chapel service the night before the game to address what they described as "the weakness within." The service was the idea of Washington head coach Joe Gibbs.

Washington, D.C., schools reported absenteeism of 50% on the day of the celebration rally for the Redskins. At Ballou High School, only 400 of 1,936 students showed up.

Super Bowl XXIII

GAME SUMMARY

January 22, 1989
Joe Robbie Stadium
Miami, Florida

This game featured a match-up of former Cincinnati quarterbacks coach Bill Walsh and his former quarterback and assistant coach Sam Wyche. With 39 seconds left in the game, San Francisco quarterback Joe Montana completed a 10-yard touchdown pass to wide receiver John Taylor. 49ers wide receiver Jerry Rice caught 11 passes for a Super Bowl-record 215 yards and was named game MVP.

I am not going to apologize for being in the Super Bowl.

Reggie Williams
Cincinnati linebacker and Cincinnati city councilman, on missing a council meeting during Super Bowl preparations

I have Super Bowl tickets. Will trade for a reliable car or truck.

Classified Ad
placed in the Miami Herald

Sam is the most brilliant coach in the NFL.

Bill Walsh
San Francisco head coach, on Cincinnati head coach Sam Wyche

I coached him four years and developed him to the upper reaches of mediocrity.

Bill Walsh
San Francisco head coach, on Sam Wyche as a quarterback with the Bengals when Walsh was a Cincinnati assistant coach

10   15   20

San Francisco 49ers	3	0	3	14	**20**
Cincinnati Bengals	0	3	10	3	**16**

Head Coaches	Bill Walsh, Sam Wyche
MVP	Jerry Rice *San Francisco wide receiver*

... *any coach who gets into [coaching] with the Super Bowl as his only goal is crazy. You have to have a whole system of things to make it happen, the way San Francisco does now. It's not the best coach; it's the best system.*

John McKay

Former coach of the Tampa Bay Buccaneers who led his team to the NFC Championship Game in 1979

It's just like getting the wind knocked out of you.

Dick Anderson

Head of Miami's Super Bowl host committee and former Miami Dolphin, on two days of riots in Overton, near Miami, which happened coincidentally during Super Bowl week

They rolled a refrigerator in front of the bus and started throwing rocks.

John Madden

Television announcer and former coach, on damage done to his Maddencruiser bus during the Overton riots

Obviously our lack of a black head coach does bother me.

Pete Rozelle

NFL Commissioner

We drove by a filling station in our bus and people ran out of the station and started doing the 'Ickey Shuffle.'

Sam Wyche

Cincinnati head coach, on Cincinnati running back Ickey Woods' touchdown dance

SIDELINE

The pregame show featured a tribute to NASA and the Kennedy Space Center. 8 astronauts from the four main phases of America's space program— Mercury, Gemini, Apollo and the Space Shuttle— appeared in person, along with space vehicles such as the Lunar Rover.

Joe Robbie, owner of the Miami Dolphins, took out a $115 million mortgage on the team to finance Joe Robbie Stadium. It is the only privately funded stadium in the league.

Super Bowl XXIII

*E*ven if I were the CEO of Procter and Gamble, I wouldn't want to live in Cincinnati.

Bill Brennan
San Francisco resident

San Francisco could come to mind.

Ronald Reagan
outgoing President of the United States, commenting on his favorite in the Super Bowl

The greatest talent I've ever seen at the quarterback position was Greg Cook.

Bill Walsh
San Francisco head coach, describing a quarterback whose six-year career with Cincinnati was ended by injury in 1974

*W*e plan to show up for all four quarters. Our guys took a vote.

Sam Wyche
Cincinnati head coach, on the Bengals' underdog role

He's the kind of guy that you have to put in a cage before the game.

Ed Brady
Cincinnati linebacker, on Bengals nose tackle Tim Krumrie

I don't know if it's important to score first. Now, if you score first, second and third, that's another thing.

Bill Walsh
San Francisco head coach

I heard somebody screaming, 'We got 'em!' I yelled, 'Will you see if number 16 is in the huddle?' He said, 'Yeah.' I said, 'Then we haven't got 'em …'

Cris Collinsworth
Cincinnati wide receiver, referring to San Francisco's Joe Montana, #16

Attendance	75,129
Top Ticket Price	$100
TV Average Share	68

I remember waiting to start that series, feeling very uptight. Joe came over and said, 'Hey, Harris. Check it out. Look–there's John Candy.' I looked and, sure enough, he was. We both laughed, then the referee blew his whistle and Joe said,

(continued)

'Okay, guys. Let's go.' He was totally cool, totally in command.

Harris Barton
San Francisco offensive tackle, on his conversation with Joe Montana before beginning the final drive that won the game for the 49ers

20 Halfback Curl, X Up.

Joe Montana
San Francisco quarterback, calling the final 49ers play– a touchdown

Joe Montana is not human. I don't want to call him a god, but he's definitely somewhere in between.

Cris Collinsworth
Cincinnati wide receiver

END ZONE

During halftime a 3-D softdrink ad was aired. 3-D viewing glasses were available in stores in the weeks before the game.

Les Boatwright, a "crazed out 49ers fan to the end," attended game XXIII in an urn. He had died six days before the game, but knowing how important it was to him, his sons attended the game with his ashes. His wife, Midge, said, "When the 49ers pulled the game out, I knew it was Les who did it–his spirit–as much as Montana or Rice."

15   10   5

Composite Standings

	W	L	PCT	PTS	OP
Pittsburgh Steelers	4	0	1.000	103	73
San Francisco 49ers	4	0	1.000	139	63
Green Bay Packers	2	0	1.000	68	24
New York Giants	2	0	1.000	59	39
Chicago Bears	1	0	1.000	46	10
New York Jets	1	0	1.000	16	7
Oakland/Los Angeles Raiders	3	1	.750	111	66
Washington Redskins	2	2	.500	85	79
Baltimore Colts	1	1	.500	23	29
Kansas City Chiefs	1	1	.500	33	42
Dallas Cowboys	2	3	.400	112	85
Miami Dolphins	2	3	.400	74	103
Buffalo Bills	0	1	.000	19	20
Los Angeles Rams	0	1	.000	19	31
New England Patriots	0	1	.000	10	46
Philadelphia Eagles	0	1	.000	10	27
Cincinnati Bengals	0	2	.000	37	46
Denver Broncos	0	4	.000	50	163
Minnesota Vikings	0	4	.000	34	95

TIME OUT

Head Coaches' Records

	W	L	PCT	YRS
Chuck Noll *Pittsburgh Steelers*	4	0	1.000	75, 76, 79, 80
Bill Walsh *San Francisco 49ers*	3	0	1.000	82, 85, 89
Tom Flores *Oakland/Los Angeles Raiders*	2	0	1.000	81, 84
Vince Lombardi *Green Bay Packers*	2	0	1.000	67, 68
Bill Parcells *New York Giants*	2	0	1.000	87, 91
Mike Ditka *Chicago Bears*	1	0	1.000	86
Weeb Ewbank *New York Jets*	1	0	1.000	69
John Madden *Oakland Raiders*	1	0	1.000	77
Don McCafferty *Baltimore Colts*	1	0	1.000	71
George Seifert *San Francisco 49ers*	1	0	1.000	90
Joe Gibbs *Washington Redskins*	2	1	.666	83, 84, 88
Hank Stram *Kansas City Chiefs*	1	1	.500	67, 70
Tom Landry *Dallas Cowboys*	2	3	.400	71, 72, 76, 78, 79
Don Shula *Baltimore Colts, Miami Dolphins*	2	4	.333	69, 72, 73, 74, 83, 85
George Allen *Washington Redskins*	0	1	.000	73
Raymond Berry *New England Patriots*	0	1	.000	86
Forrest Gregg *Cincinnati Bengals*	0	1	.000	82
Marv Levy *Buffalo Bills*	0	1	.000	91
Ray Malavasi *Los Angeles Rams*	0	1	.000	80
Red Miller *Denver Broncos*	0	1	.000	78
John Rauch *Oakland Raiders*	0	1	.000	68
Dick Vermeil *Philadelphia Eagles*	0	1	.000	81
Sam Wyche *Cincinnati Bengals*	0	1	.000	89
Dan Reeves *Denver Broncos*	0	3	.000	87, 88, 90
Bud Grant *Minnesota Vikings*	0	4	.000	70, 74, 75, 77

Super Bowl XXIV

GAME SUMMARY

January 28, 1990
Louisiana Superdome
New Orleans, Louisiana

The 49ers dominated the Broncos. San Francisco's 55 points, as well as their 45-point victory margin, were records. Joe Montana completed 22 of 29 pass attempts for 297 yards and five touchdowns and was named game MVP a record third time.

This win tied the 49ers and Pittsburgh Steelers with 4 Super Bowl victories each.

Super Bowl 24. There it is in print with the more familiar Arabic numbers. Written this way, it certainly seems less like a monumental event, and more like something from the inventory list of a plumbing supply house.

Robert Klein
Comedian

We're looking for a return to the wild, wild West. John throwing, John scrambling, us scoring.

Mark Jackson
Denver receiver,
referring to quarterback
John Elway

We're reminded every day by people in the press that we don't have a chance. But we do.

Dan Reeves
Denver
head coach

San Francisco 49ers	13	14	14	14	**55**
Denver Broncos	3	0	7	0	**10**

Head Coaches George Seifert, Dan Reeves

MVP Joe Montana *San Francisco quarterback*

They didn't want anything to do with us. I was kind of surprised. I mean, we can at least be cordial to each other.

Spencer Tillman

San Francisco running back, after a group of Broncos players refused a friendly drink with several 49ers in the French Quarter

[Elway's] problem is he's been babied by the city until this year. He's been babied by the coach. Is he a great quarterback? No. He's very good but he's too inconsistent. He's too-too-too inconsistent.

Terry Bradshaw

Television announcer and former Pittsburgh Steeler quarterback

He sounds to me like a jealous man. Why would Bradshaw say something like that? John must have beat him at golf.

Vance Johnson

Denver receiver, defending John Elway

He's jealous of my money. He's jealous of my hair.

John Elway

Denver quarterback, responding to Terry Bradshaw's criticism

SIDELINE

CBS' pre-game show, trying to build a case for the underdog Broncos, featured film clips of Super Bowl III's upset, the 1980 U.S. hockey team's miracle win over the Soviets, and clips from against-all-odd-movies such as Hoosiers and Rocky II. The San Francisco front office had a box of game III clippings to remind the 49ers not to take the Broncos too lightly.

Some 2,800 media credentials were issued for game XXIV. Super Bowl I had issued 338.

Super Bowl XXIV

49ers' 55-10 Win is Big, Easy

USA Today headline on January 29

Joe Montana is such a surgeon the other teams don't have much chance.

Pat Summerall
Television announcer

The only thing Denver won was the coin toss.

Randy Cross
Former San Francisco center and veteran of three Super Bowls

With a 27-3 score, assistant coaches in the press box start eating hot dogs earlier than usual.

John Madden
Television announcer, referring to the game's halftime score

This is the worst nightmare. This is worse than anyone ever predicted.

Jim Brown
Manager of Brooklyn's bar in Denver

Now we can be mentioned in the same breath with Pittsburgh, Miami, the Green Bay Packers. A team from Mars could have come down here, and it wouldn't have mattered; no one could have stepped in our way.

Roger Craig
San Francisco running back

Everything they did, we knew about. We just couldn't stop 'em.

Tyrone Braxton
Denver defensive back

Matt Millen (helping John Elway to his feet): Hang in there. It's a tough one.

Elway: You got that right.

Exchange between the San Francisco linebacker and Denver quarterback, recalled by Elway after the game

Attendance	72,919	
Top Ticket Price	$125	
TV Average Share	63	

Well, I might be dumb, but I ain't stupid. There's no need to look again.

Dan Reeves
Denver coach, when asked if he had watched a tape of the game

It got to the point where, being a Christian and being a person who loves people, I actually felt sorry for the Broncos.

Bubba Paris
San Francisco offensive tackle

Would the Steelers have beat the 49ers? What do you want me to say? Of course they would.

Terry Bradshaw
Television announcer and retired quarterback of the Pittsburgh Steelers, winners of four Super Bowls

I still have my hair.

Joe Montana
San Francisco quarterback, asked to compare himself to Terry Bradshaw

God would have had trouble beating them today. In fact, they had God today.

Pat Bowlen
Denver owner, referring to San Francisco quarterback Joe Montana

I'm still trying to figure out how to win one, or at least be in one.

John Elway
Denver quarterback

END ZONE

A framed picture taken by Jennifer Montana of her and Joe's 3 children showed up in his locker on game day. In it Alexandra and Elizabeth each wore one of Joe's Super Bowl rings on her thumb and baby Nathaniel had his pinned to his 49ers T-shirt. An inscription read, "OK, Daddy. The next ring is yours."

Denver Broncos coach Dan Reeves has competed in eight Super Bowls as a player, assistant coach and head coach— more than any other individual.

Super Bowl XXV

GAME SUMMARY

January 27, 1991
Tampa Stadium
Tampa, Florida

In a well-played game with no turnovers, Matt Bahr's 21-yard field goal set the Giants up for victory as Buffalo placekicker Scott Norwood missed a 47-yard field goal with 8 seconds remaining in the game. Ottis Anderson was named MVP for his 102 yards on 21 carries. The Bills' "no-huddle offense" was led by quarterback Jim Kelly. Jeff Hostetler led the Giants after Super Bowl XXI MVP Phil Simms was injured late in the regular season.

UPDATE

The threat of terrorism prompted extraordinary security measures at Tampa Stadium, including installation of a concrete barrier and chainlink fence around the stadium. Fans were required to pass through metal detectors, handbags were searched and car trunks were examined. No electronic devices, umbrellas, coolers, bottles or cans were allowed. Stadium airspace was declared off-limits and the Goodyear Blimp was banned from its usual overhead view of the game.

This week, only one story counts, and clearly it won't be about a football game.

Leonard Shapiro
Washington Post

I'll watch. But life isn't in sync.

Roger Staubach
Retired Dallas Cowboys quarterback who also served four years in Vietnam, referring to the Persian Gulf War

New York Giants	3	7	7	3	**20**
Buffalo Bills	3	9	0	7	**19**

Head Coaches	Bill Parcells, Marv Levy
MVP	Ottis Anderson *New York running back*

It'll be important that the Giants win, but it'll be more important to live than to see them do it.

*Captain
Diane Merritt*

In Saudi Arabia
commenting on the
possibility of an Iraqi
attack during the
broadcast

Iraq won the toss and elected to receive.

Roadsign

in Cincinnati, Ohio
on Super Bowl Sunday

Football playerspeak is filled with war analogies. Bomb. Blitz. Assault. Aerial attack. These words are so out of place ... considering what's happening over there.

Bob Sansevere

Sportswriter
St. Paul Pioneer
Press-Dispatch

I think people back home ought to go about business as usual, and we'll take care of business over here.

*Staff Sergeant
Doug Kline*

In Dhahran, Saudi
Arabia, when asked if he
thought the Super Bowl
should be cancelled
because of the war

... unusually quiet.

Peter Jennings

ABC-News, reporting
between the first and
second quarters on the
scene in the Gulf region
where it was 3 a.m. with
a nearly-full moon

SIDELINE

Troops in Saudi Arabia had to settle for non-alcoholic beer during the game because of Muslim restrictions on alcohol. Most were ordered to wear bulky chemical protective suits and keep gasmasks at hand in case of an attack.

On a war update during the pre-game show, a military analyst drew on a map with an illustration technique developed for football replays.

Super Bowl XXV

The last *M*A*S*H* show was a headache too, but this could be the greatest challenge of all.

George Marlle

Erie County Water Authority (Buffalo, New York) supervising production engineer on the large amount of water used by television viewers during Super Bowl timeouts

We've got a no-rodent policy.

Security man at the Tampa Convention Center explaining to Minnie and Mickey Mouse that they would not be allowed into the media work area for security reasons

I'm not Superman, but I'm happy being Clark Kent. Clark Kent can get the job done.

Lawrence Taylor

New York linebacker, on his diminishing skills

We have a rule that our backs don't fumble, because if they do they will be someone else's backs.

Bill Parcells

New York head coach

I was thinking, 'Please go through.'

Jim Kelly

Buffalo quarterback, on Scott Norwood's field goal attempt late in the game

It wasn't moving; it wasn't being drawn in.

Scott Norwood

Buffalo placekicker, on his missed field goal with 8 seconds left in the game

When it's too tough for them, it's just right for us.

Motto of the Buffalo Bills

No other team ever hit me this hard. You can't even compare this to anything I've ever been through.

Andre Reed

Buffalo wide receiver

Attendance	73,813
Top Ticket Price	$150
TV Average Share	63

I broke my face mask on Anderson in the first half. It just snapped and turned all the way around to the right side of my helmet. I mean, jeez, it's the first time I ever broke a face mask.

Shane Conlan
Buffalo linebacker

*W*hether football [is] the moral equivalent of war, or war the immoral equivalent of football, they certainly [speak] the same language.

Tom Callahan
U.S. News &
World Report

*T*he Super Bowl has become the winter version of the Fourth of July celebration.

Paul Tagliabue
NFL Commissioner

It's a little piece of home.

Air Force
Lieutenant
Kate Mangion
in Saudi Arabia
on the Super Bowl

END ZONE

Super Bowl XXV tickets were the first sports tickets to feature a hologram. It showed the stadium and the Vince Lombardi Trophy and made the ticket stub an instant collectible worth $75.

Ticket scalpers were selling an end-zone ticket for $450 and a seat on the 50-yard line for $1,500.

Super Bowl XXV was watched by some 120 million people in the United States and 750 million people worldwide.

39-20
Ouch.

42-10
Ouch!

We came, we saw,
we kicked their butts.

YEAR

55-10
OUCH!

Index

Waters, Charlie, **21**, 59

A quote by the person
is shown by a bold number.

A quote *about* the person
is shown by a light number.

Fernandez, Manny, **35**
Ferragamo, Vince, 65
Fleming, Marv, **9**, **32**, 59
Flores, Tom, **69**, 69, **83**, 83, **84**, 85, 111
Fouts, Dan, 37
Francis, Russ, **91**
Fugett, Jean, **47**
Fuqua, John, **40**

Galbreath, Tony, **98**
Galimore, Willie, 95
Garcia, Francisco, **33**
Garrison, Walt, 26
Gaye, Marvin, 39
George, Bill, 95
Gerela, Roy, 44, 46
Gibbs, Joe, 61, 79, **81**, 81, 83, 103, 104, 105, 111
Gifford, Frank, **4**
Gillingham, Gale, 4
Gillman, Esther, **7**
Gillman, Sid, 7, **21**
Graham, Billy, 27
Graham, Otto, 81
Grambling University Band, 39
Grange, Red, 9
Grant, Bud, **16**, 17, **18**, **19**, **34**, 35, **37**, **41**, 41, 51, **52**, **53**, 53, 111
Greene, (Mean) Joe, **40**, **42**, **43**, 87
Greenwood, L.C., 87
Gregg, Forrest, 9, 69, 75, 86, 111
Griese, Bob, **26**, 36, 37
Grimm, Russ, 79, **82**
Guy, Ray, 87

Halas, George, 3, 23, 51, 61, 95
Halftime events, 17, 31, 69, 93, 99, 109

Ham, Jack, 43, 87
Harris, Cliff, **45**, 46, **59**, 59
Harris, Franco, 40, 41, **43**, 45, 47, 86
Harrison, Reggie, 44, **47**
Hawkins, Alex, **10**
Hayes, Lester, **70**
Hegman, Mike, 58
Henderson, Thomas (Hollywood), **44**, **46**, **56**, **59**, **60**, 60, **61**, 61
Hendricks, Ted, 68, 87
Hewitt, Bill, 95
Hill, Jerry, 10
Hill, Kenny, **99**
Hill, Tony, 58
Hirt, Al, 39
Holmes, Ernie (Fats), **44**
Holub, E.J., **2**
Holy Angels School Choir, 39
Hostetler, Jeff, 116
Houston, Jim, 16
Houston, Whitney, 39
Howley, Chuck, 21
Hunley, Ricky, **102**
Hunt, Lamar, vi, 3, 51

Jackson, Mark, 103, **112**
Jaworski, Ron, **70**, **71**
Jenkins, Dan, **50**, **51**, 57
Jennings, Peter, **117**
Jensen, Derrick, 82
Jesus, 45
Joel, Billy, 39
Johnson, Butch, 54
Johnson, Pete, **77**, 77
Johnson, Vance, **103**, **113**
Jones, Ed (Too Tall), **75**, 87
Jordan, Henry, **9**
Jordan, Leroy, **21**

Kapp, Joe, 16, **17**, **18**, **19**
Karlis, Rich, **100**, 101
Karras, Alex, **51**
Keating, Tom, **8**
Kelly, Jim, 116, **118**
Kelly, Phyllis, 39
Kiick, Jim, **32**, 37
King, Kenny, 68
Klein, Robert, **112**
Kline, Doug, **117**
Knox, Chuck, 61
Kornheiser, Tony, **66**, **84**, **90**
Kramer, Jerry, **3**, **4**, **9**, 86
Krause, Paul, **53**
Krumrie, Tim, 108
Kuechenberg, Bob, **30**

Ladd, Cheryl, 39
Lambeau, Earl (Curly), 81
Lambert, Jack, **44**, 44, **46**, 66, 87
Lamonica, Daryle, **8**
Landry, Tom, 21, **22**, 23, **27**, 27, 45, 47, 54, 55, 59, **60**, 93, 111
Langer, Jim, 30
Lanier, Willie, **18**
Levy, Marv, 111, 117
Lewis, D.D., 59
Lilly, Bob, **22**, **29**
Littwin, Mike, 78
Lombardi, Marie, **5**, **6**, 68
Lombardi, Vince, vii, **2**, **3**, 3, **4**, 4, **5**, 5, **6**, **7**, **8**, **9**, 9, 68, 81, 86, 111
Long, Howie, **54**, 83
Lott, Ronnie, 76, 87, 91
Luckman, Sid, 95
Lundquist, Verne, **60**

Another head-bobbling book
in the **War Of The Words** series

War Of The Words:
The Gulf War Quote By Quote